SOVEREIGN LIVING I
A WOMAN'S GUIDE TO RECLAIMING YOUR
CROWN

LAURA ALFANO

Sovereign Living I
A Woman's Guide to Reclaiming Your Crown

Laura Alfano

Copyright © 2026 Laura Alfano
All rights reserved

Laura Alfano
Alfano, Inc.
Malibu, California
LauraAlfano22@gmail.com
LauraAlfano.com

No part of this publication may be reproduced, distributed or transmitted in any form or by any means, including photocopying, recording, or other electronic or mechanical methods, without the prior written permission of the publisher, except in the case of brief quotations embodied in critical reviews and certain other noncommercial uses permitted by copyright law.

For permission requests, sales to U.S. bookstores and wholesalers, or to inquire about quantity discounts, please contact the publisher at the email address above.

Library of Congress Control Number: 2025923707

ISBN – 979-8-9938449-0-9

First Edition
10 9 8 7 6 5 4 3 2 1

Printed in the United States of America

SOVEREIGN LIVING I
A WOMAN'S GUIDE TO RECLAIMING YOUR
CROWN

DEDICATION

This book is dedicated to my
three beautiful children and
their children, to my endlessly
patient parents, to my irreplaceable
siblings, and Alfano, Inc. You are all
a vital part of the legacy of love
that lives in these pages.

CONTENT

PART ONE - RECOGNITION............1
   Crisis to Willful Change 3
   Fear to Love................................. 11
   Head to Heart 19
   Separation to ONE 25
   Serve Others to Serving Self, First 31
   Holding Guilt & Shame to Becoming
   Vulnerable 37
   Addiction to Awareness 43
   Conditional to Unconditional Love............ 49
   Projecting to Protecting 55
   Decision Making from the Subconscious to Free
   Will 61
   Avoidance to Engagement 69
   Know Thy Self to Knowing Thy Self........... 75
   Karma to Dharma............................ 81
   Impatience to Patient........................ 87
   Turbulence to Stillness....................... 93
   Heaven to Earth 99
   Possessions to Gifts 105
   Resist to Surrender.......................... 111

PART TWO - QUEENSHIP 117
   Woman to Women 119
   Servant to Queen 125
   Jealousy to Admiration 133
   Damsel in Distress to Wonder Woman 139

Giving to Receiving 145
Indecisive to Internal Knowing 151
Perception to Reality 155
Identity Crisis to Identity Creation 161
Judgment to Judgment Detox. 165
Seeking Happiness to Being Happiness 171
Blind to Seeing 177
Wearing Clothes to Curating a Signature Look . 183

PART THREE - MANIFESTATION 191
Manifesting from Neptune in Pisces to
Neptune in Aries 193
Limited Beliefs to Limitless Possibilities. 199
Dreamer to Doer. 205
Wandering to Wanderlust 211
Perfection to Passion 217
Loss to Gratitude 223
Scarcity to Abundance. 229
Cluttered Mind to Laser-Focused Desire 235
Distraction to Intentional Action 241
Obsession with an Idea to Planting the Seed
of Desire. 247
Resistance to Persistence. 253
Bird's Eye View to Spy Plane View 257
Pessimism to Optimism 263
No to a Resounding *Yes!* 269
Release to Expand 275

AUTHOR'S NOTE

Dearest Reader,

Sovereign Living is an invitation to return home to yourself. It is not about perfection or performance but about alignment, living in harmony with your truth, your boundaries, and your deepest values. This book will help you recognize where you have given away your power and show you how to reclaim it with grace, clarity, and confidence.

This is more than a story; it is a lifeline. It shares my real and raw journey through life's firestorms, sometimes running, often walking, and in certain seasons, crawling, but always moving forward. These lessons were not learned in comfort; they were earned through heartbreak, courage, and perseverance. Each one became a stepping stone toward Sovereignty, and they can become yours too.

As you turn each page, let my voice steady you and my story remind you that you are not alone. I have been where you are and perhaps where you dare to go. I am here to guide you, believe in you, and walk this path with you.

A Call to Reclaim Your Sovereignty

For a woman, ***Sovereign Living*** is about unlearning dependence, reclaiming power, and defining life through her own inner authority rather than societal expectation. You were born Sovereign; it is your birthright.

This series of three books is a call to reclaim your Sovereignty: ***your Crown, your Heart, and your***

Compass. It reminds you that you are the ultimate authority in your life and invites you to rise in your own dominion. Each chapter offers a new perspective to help you move from self-doubt to self-mastery, from external validation to inner peace, and from autopilot to intention.

Sovereign Living invites you to step fully into your power and become the creator of your own life. Here, you will stand rooted in your truth, make decisions aligned with your soul, and create boundaries that honor your energy and well-being. You will be called to release outdated beliefs, shed conditioning, and let go of the need for approval. Instead, you will learn to trust your intuition, honor your desires, and take bold steps toward the life you deserve.

What Is Sovereign Living?

At its core, *Sovereign Living I: A Woman's Guide to Reclaiming Your Crown* is about embodying self-governance in every aspect of your life: emotional, spiritual, physical, and mental. It means standing firm in your values and beliefs, regardless of external expectations.

It is cultivating confidence and grace through every challenge and realizing that peace and happiness are not given by others but found within the deep well of wisdom and love already living inside you.

Sovereignty means living in alignment, connected to your truth, your purpose, and your deepest desires. It is not about power over others but about self-mastery and freedom from external validation. It is recognizing your worth, embracing your potential, and allowing yourself to thrive.

How to Use This Book

This book is meant to meet you where you are. You can read it from beginning to end or open to a chapter that speaks to your current experience. There are three parts organized by theme, and each stands on its own. One chapter a day may be all you have time for, and that is enough. You will receive what you need, exactly when you need it.

Each chapter of *Sovereign Living* is designed to guide your transformation. Consider this book a trusted companion on your journey, a way to awaken the Sovereign self within.

By way of my stories, self-inquiry exercises (*Reflect / Reframe / Reconnect*), journaling prompts, and mindful practices, you will uncover truths buried beneath layers of doubt, fear, and confusion. These practices are not meant to change who you are but to help you remember who you have always been.

Through the wisdom and insights shared in *Sovereign Living I: A Woman's Guide to Reclaiming Your Crown*, you will be guided through three parts of transformation:

Part One: Recognition awakens you to love, releases fear, and reconnects you with your innate wisdom.

Part Two: Queenship empowers you to step into your authority, rooted in strength, grace, and self-leadership.

Part Three: Manifestation brings vision to life as your Sovereign essence shines boldly in the world.

Each section calls you to ascend to your Crown, remembering your strength, reclaiming your authority, and embodying the confidence that comes from inner alignment. Together, these parts help you stand in your power, lead with integrity, and live as the Sovereign of your own life.

Why Sovereignty Matters

In a world that feels chaotic and uncertain, Sovereignty is the foundation of peace. It is the grounding force that allows you to live with authenticity and freedom.

No matter where you are in your journey, this book will help you release the barriers that have kept you from stepping into your full potential. You do not need permission to be your most confident, authentic, and powerful self. You were born to lead your life with intention, courage, and clarity.

Everything you need already exists within you.

As Glinda said to Dorothy in *The Wizard of Oz*, "You have always had the power, my dear; you just had to learn it for yourself."

This is your time to live Sovereign, to stand in your truth, to step into your power, and to become the woman you were always meant to be.

Welcome to **Sovereign Living**, a journey back to yourself.

Let's get started,

Laura

INTRODUCTION

Sovereign [sov-rin]
  1. **a monarch; a supreme ruler.**
  Related Words: **absolute, autonomous, unlimited, self-governing, clear, true**

The dictionary offers a strong foundation for the word *Sovereign*, but now, it's time to expand its meaning to reflect the power, grace, and presence of the **Sovereign Woman** of today.

A **Sovereign Woman** is the absolute ruler of her own life.

A **Sovereign Woman** stands rooted in her own truth.

A **Sovereign Woman** creates boundaries that honor her own well-being.

A **Sovereign Woman** is the guardian of her energy.

A **Sovereign Woman** is released from outdated beliefs, societal conditioning, and need for approval from others.

A **Sovereign Woman** trusts her intuition, honors her desires, and takes bold steps toward the life she deserves.

In your heart, do you feel the qualities of a **Sovereign Woman** alive within you today? If not, trust that you can and you will. This book was written to guide you there. In truth, my life has been a continual journey to understand and embody that power. I've come a long way, and the learning continues. I share these experiences with the hope that something within them will inspire you.

Sovereign Living means embracing your inner Queen.

Sovereign Living means reclaiming your individual identity, your inner voice, your personal truth, and your full power.

Sovereign Living means aligning your words and actions with your values, desires, and passions.

Sovereign Living means releasing judgment of yourself and others.

Sovereign Living is the absolute power to manifest your desires, not by struggle but naturally and with ease.

Each chapter of ***Sovereign Living I: A Woman's Guide to Reclaiming Your Crown*** is designed to guide you forward in your own transformation. My wish is that this book becomes a trusted companion on your journey to awaken the Sovereign self within you. You'll find practical tools and mindful practices to help you uncover truths you've buried beneath layers of doubt, fear, and confusion.

These practices are not meant to change who you are. They are meant to help you remember who you've always been and become the **Sovereign Woman** you are meant to be.

Part One

RECOGNITION
CHOOSING LOVE, HEALING FEAR & AWAKENING WISDOM

Recognition is the sacred act of remembering, of returning to your essence after years of forgetting. It is the moment you choose love over fear, wisdom over illusion, and wholeness over separation. To reclaim your Crown, you must awaken to who you truly are.

In **Crisis to Willful Change**, you discover that awakening often begins in breakdown, when life shakes the foundation so you can rebuild in truth. Fear becomes a doorway to courage, and resistance softens into surrender.

Fear to Love guides you into the heart's intelligence, where openness replaces defense and trust grows stronger than control. In **Head to Heart**, you descend from analysis to alignment, learning to follow intuition instead of logic.

In **Separation to ONE**, you dissolve the illusion of division and remember your unity with all life. **Serve Others to Serving Self, First** reframes service as self-honoring, a devotion that begins within and radiates outward.

Through **Holding Guilt & Shame to Becoming Vulnerable**, you learn that transparency is not weakness but liberation. Healing begins when you meet yourself with tenderness. In **Addiction to Awareness**, you awaken from numbing patterns to presence, turning avoidance into agency.

Conditional to Unconditional Love reminds you that love is not earned but expressed. In **Projecting to Protecting**, you stop giving away power and begin safeguarding peace, shifting from blame to responsibility.

Decision Making from the Subconscious to Free Will reveals how awareness transforms reaction into intention. **Avoidance to Engagement** teaches that growth requires participation with life.

Through **Know Thy Self to Knowing Thy Self**, wisdom deepens from concept to embodiment. In **Karma to Dharma**, you transform repetition into revelation, aligning with purpose rather than pain. **Impatience to Patience** teaches trust in divine timing, while **Turbulence to Stillness** anchors you in calm amid life's motion.

In **Heaven to Earth**, you learn to live your divinity through the ordinary. **Possessions to Gifts** transforms attachment into appreciation, revealing abundance as gratitude, not accumulation.

Finally, in **Resist to Surrender**, you arrive at freedom. Surrender becomes your Crown, the moment you stop controlling life and begin co-creating with it.

Recognition is where awakening begins, the bridge from illusion to embodiment, from survival to Sovereignty. Each step toward love brings you home to yourself, whole, radiant, and free.

CRISIS TO WILLFUL CHANGE

> *"A crisis exists for you to have victory over it."*
> ~ *Guru Jagat*

Crisis is the beginning of a transformation. It's like the opening of a cocoon, the first tremble of silk before wings unfurl. It's the hush before a butterfly remembers it was meant to fly. The metamorphosis has already begun; the colors are there, the breeze is waiting. But will you take flight?

Some linger, clinging to the tattered threads of what was. Others flap once, then fold back in, unsure of the sky. And some, dazzled by the new light, begin to write poems about flying, without ever leaving the branch.

When a crisis occurs in your life, have you ever asked yourself, "Why is this happening to me?" That's a question of someone who feels powerless, caught in a victim mindset by unconscious choices, unhealed wounds, and forgotten boundaries.

But we are never merely victims of circumstance, because we are always in control of how we respond. If your house is burned down in a wildfire you're not responsible for that event. But what you are in control of is how you respond. Do you feel sorry for yourself and stay stuck, or do you start building a new house? The choice is yours, and only yours.

Radical accountability for your choices is the first step toward Sovereignty. You have to take that step. You can't move forward without it.

What Is a Crisis?

It's a shocking, unexpected break that cracks the familiar rhythm of life. It can arrive as a physical event or a sudden realization. It knocks the wind out of you and strips away any illusion of control, leaving you standing there, asking yourself, "What now?"

Author Bruce Feiler, in his book *Life Is in the Transitions: Mastering Change at Any Age*, calls these moments "lifequakes." They are disruptive yet transformative periods that shake the foundation of our lives. He reminds us that these upheavals, while often painful, are not just endings; they are invitations to rebuild with greater truth, resilience, and purpose.

My Story: Transforming a Crisis

A crisis often arrives when you've ignored subtle invitations to change. But it doesn't have to define us. With conscious reflection, a shift in perspective, and deliberate reconnection to truth, you can move from crisis to clarity.

A crisis can expose the gap between the life you've been living and the life you're meant to live. That message came for me when my brother passed away. I suddenly felt small, like I'd been going through life half-asleep. It shattered something in me and it exposed something else.

I had been checking all the right boxes, meeting expectations, and missing the whole point. My brother's untimely death forced me to ask deeper questions:

- What am I doing with my one-and-only precious life?
- What is my purpose?
- What kind of legacy will I leave?

I had always told myself I was fine. I was a mother, and wasn't that enough? But something inside me said no. Not because motherhood isn't sacred; it is one of the greatest legacies we create. But our children are not the whole of our legacy. Legacy is not only lineage; it is impact. Their lives are their own. And while they will always be part of the imprint I leave on this world, I could feel myself being called to grow in ways I could not yet name.

When I wrote my brother's eulogy, I had a revelation. His life had been both beautiful and difficult. As I searched for the words to describe him I felt myself reconnecting to something raw and essential, not just in him, but also in me.

After the death of my younger brother, writing his eulogy became a form of catharsis. Grief turned into energy, burning through everything I had avoided, including my marriage. In that tender clarity, I was forced to take inventory of my life, every choice, every silence, and every part of myself I had tucked away for the sake of keeping the peace. None of this was planned, as one crisis revealed another, and both became turning points.

I loved my life. I was deeply fulfilled as a mother, grateful for a successful career, surrounded by good friends, family, and the comforts I had worked hard to build. Yet beneath it all, I felt an ache I could no longer ignore. I didn't know how to ask for a divorce, and I didn't know how to mend what felt irreparably broken. So I froze. That emotional paralysis became its own crisis, the quiet unraveling of my marriage and the beginning of a reckoning I could no longer postpone.

From Crisis to Courageous Change

Crisis alone does not create transformation. Instead, crisis offers you a choice. You can collapse back into the old, or rise into the new. Making the correct choice requires self-awareness, intention, and courage to hear the inner voice that already knows the way.

To emerge victorious in a crisis:

- Pause. When shock hits, breathe. Give your nervous system time to settle.
- Zoom out. Look at the big picture. Break it down into manageable steps. What needs your attention in the next few hours? The next few days?
- Stay calm. Whether you're navigating loss, heartbreak, or sudden change, remind yourself: You are still here. You will be okay.
- Reach out. Don't isolate yourself. Call your support system. Let people witness and support you.
- Seek guidance that helps you see with new eyes, whether legal, financial, or emotional, and walk beside wisdom as you navigate the path ahead.
- Take accountability. Where were the signs? Did you override your intuition? Be honest with yourself without blaming yourself.

- Feel the emotions. Don't numb or bypass them. Let the pain rise, feel it, observe it and release it.
- Begin again. When you're ready, shift your focus toward healing, reinvention, and take actions that align with victory.

Recognizing Crisis Before It Hits

Your intuition of a crisis is like a traffic light:

- Green Light (Whisper): A soft inner voice says, "Something feels off." You ignore it and keep going without paying much attention to the warning from your intuition.
- Yellow Light (Tap): The discomfort grows. You feel tension. Doubt creeps in. You slow down, think more about it, and just keep going.
- Red Light (Crash): You ignored the whispers. You ignored the taps. Either you full stop or life hits the breaks for you.

This is the moment of reckoning, and your greatest opportunity. You can crash again, or you can course-correct, heal, and grow.

So sit with the pain. Listen to what it's asking of you. Let it shape you into someone wiser, deeper, and more free.

Reflect

Awareness is the first tool for transformation. By looking back without judgment, you prepare to move forward with intention.

- Recall your last personal crisis. What triggered it and how did you react emotionally, physically, or spiritually?
- Were there signs beforehand? Did your body, intuition, or environment try to warn you?
- What wisdom emerged through that experience? Did it reveal any patterns, boundary breaches, or outdated coping strategies?
- What signals did you miss? How can you listen more closely next time?

Journaling Prompt: *What was my most recent crisis trying to show me? What signals did I miss, and how can I listen more closely next time?*

Reframe

Crisis may feel like collapse, but it often clears the path for deeper alignment. When we choose to see through the lens of growth, we reclaim our power.

- A crisis is not the end; it's a threshold. A chance to realign your life with what's true and needed.
- Your breakdown could be the soil where your next breakthrough takes root.
- Crisis strips away illusion. It doesn't arrive to punish you, but to wake you up and bring you closer to wholeness.

Journal Prompt: *Instead of asking "Why is this happening to me?" Try: "What is this trying to wake up in me?"*

Reconnect

After a storm, you rebuild by returning to what's real: your values, your vision, your voice. This is where healing takes root.

- Reconnect with your inner wisdom. In stillness or reflection, ask: "What does my soul need most right now?"
- Ground yourself in simple truths: people, practices, or places that bring strength, peace, or perspective.
- Begin shaping your post-crisis vision. What will you no longer tolerate? What new boundaries or commitments will you honor moving forward?

Affirmation: *I trust that this moment is shaping me, not breaking me. I choose growth, clarity, and willful change.*

Final Thought: Let the Fire Refine You

Crisis is the fire that tests you.
You are not meant to burn.
You are meant to be forged.
You are meant to become truer.

You do not need all the answers.
You only need honesty now.
Let the loss strip illusions.
Let the rupture open you.

Let the storm clear its path.
This is not your ending.
This is your becoming.
Your future is calling forward.

It is not rushing you.
It is a reminder of your strength.
Step forward even shaky.
Rise into the self awaiting you.

This is Sovereign Living.

FEAR TO LOVE

*"Your greatest strength is love.
Your greatest weakness is fear."*
~ Yogi Bhajan

Choosing love over fear has been the greatest catalyst in my own journey toward Sovereignty, toward inner freedom, self-trust, and unshakable self-worth.

We are all born whole, pure, and miraculous. Love, the living expression of Sovereignty, is our original nature. Yet we do not arrive fully formed, not in body or in spirit. Within each of us is a constellation of potential, waiting to be illuminated through experience and awareness. Just as stars reveal their brilliance only when night falls, our deepest strength often awakens in darkness. Growth unfolds slowly, guided by both shadow and light.

When you took your first breath, you didn't yet know the language of fear or doubt. You cried out, not in despair, but in readiness, a declaration of life that said, "I'm here. Let's begin." From that moment, your journey began: to evolve, to learn, to love, and to remember the radiance that has always lived within you.

The road to love is rarely smooth. There are sharp turns, unexpected detours, and moments of uncertainty. But each one offers a lesson in returning to your true self. The practice is not about eliminating fear; it is about meeting it with compassion and choosing love anyway. That is where Sovereignty begins.

Why do we choose fear?

In every life, a wall slowly rises between the love we were born to receive and the way we learn to experience the world. That wall is built from fear.

Fear wasn't there at the beginning. It came later, usually early in life while you were still learning how to make sense of what was going on around you. Inevitably, some painful things started happening, like rejection, punishment, and unmet needs. You began to have doubt about the world and your place in it. Consciously or unconsciously, there were some scary questions: "Am I not good enough?" "Am I too much?" "Or am I not enough?"

The present-day name for this painful experience is trauma. It can take many forms. Your trauma may look inconsequential to the world at large. It may go unnoticed even by people closest to you. Or it can be a clear and obvious catastrophe: a death in the family, or serious illness. Whatever it is, trauma is probably not a strong enough word for it. Because when trauma happens to you at an early age, you experience it as a full-fledged tragedy.

It seems like no one can avoid this. If there's one thing I've noticed about people, it's how everyone has a personal tragic story. Some people are in touch with it all the time. They're aware of what happened to them and how they're trying to deal with it. For other people, this personal tragedy has been hidden even to their conscious selves, and identifying it is an important step toward healing. But one way or another, it's there:

- Death of a loved one
- Divorce or breakup with a partner

- Serious illness or injury
- Job loss or financial ruin
- Addiction (self or loved one)
- Mental health struggles (depression, anxiety)

We must never sit in judgment of the countless ways people can experience pain. In fact, I encourage you now to take a close look at an early traumatic event in your life. You've certainly got one. We all do.

Tragedy Into Triumph

When people get in touch with their early trauma it can become the center of their identity, even in a public way. They can't stop thinking about it, and maybe they can't stop talking about it either. You don't want to sit next to somebody like that at a dinner party.

Often people extend their tragic story from the past into a triumph story in the present: "We were too poor to buy a car and now I drive a Porsche!" This transformation can be a satisfying experience. But it can also be a trap if "proving the doubters wrong" is as far as you choose to go.

Sovereignty transcends tragedy and triumph. It's not denying what's happened in the past or what's happening now, but it's seeing both from a new perspective. Rudyard Kipling put this very well in his poem titled "If":

If you can dream and not make dreams your master;
If you can think and not make thoughts your aim;
If you can meet with Triumph and Disaster
And treat those two impostors just the same…

Love is the active expression of Sovereignty. You don't "feel Sovereignty" toward other people or to the world. You do feel love toward them, and even toward yourself as well. When this happens, love is often returned to you by others. But no one can give Sovereignty to you. They may recognize you as a Sovereign person, although they might not use that word. But they see what you are through what you do.

This book is not rooted in religion, but in the shared human search for meaning, connection, and truth. While many traditions have tried to define love, few words capture its depth and power as clearly as those found in *The First Letter of Paul to the Corinthians*. Though written long ago, this passage speaks timelessly to the essence of love and, by extension, to the heart of Sovereignty itself.

> *"Love is patient, love is kind.*
>
> *It does not envy, it does not boast, it is not proud.*
>
> *It does not dishonor others, it is not self-seeking, it is not easily angered, it keeps no record of wrongs.*
>
> *Love does not delight in evil but rejoices with the truth.*
>
> *It always protects, always trusts, always hopes, always perseveres.*
>
> *Love never fails. But where there are prophecies, they will cease; where there is language, it will be stilled;*
>
> *where there is knowledge, it will pass away.*
>
> *For now we know in part but when completeness comes, what is in part disappears."*

The Apostle Paul speaks simply and directly about what love is and what it is not. There is no mention of wealth or power. Yet this was composed at the height of the Roman Empire, and Paul himself was executed during the emperor Nero's reign. It's off the beaten path of the Roman period to read a sentence like, "Love is patient, love is kind." Writing something like that could get you killed, and in this case it did. It was a revolutionary sentiment that directly challenged the values of the time.

I think these passages speak for themselves, and it's worth thinking seriously about what they mean. I want to mention that the word "completeness" could also be translated as Sovereignty for our purposes. "When Sovereignty comes, what is in part disappears."

My Story: A Trauma that Shaped Fear

I was six years old. It was Good Friday so my cousins and I had been dismissed early from Catholic school. We were playing outside when we heard the ice cream truck. My mother had given me two quarters. I mistook them for nickels and thought I didn't have enough for ice cream. My cousin offered to pay, but I insisted on going back inside for more money.

When I stepped out from behind the ice cream truck, a speeding car hit me. We learned later that the car was rushing a woman in labor to the hospital.

I landed on my face. I lost eight baby teeth. I broke my jaw and my arm. My leg was also damaged.

I didn't cry. I was stoic. I was silent. Maybe I thought that crying would make it all worse. But getting hit by the car stayed with me, physically, mentally, and emotionally. For years, I didn't realize how deeply the trauma had shaped my beliefs, my fears, and my default responses to everything that went on in my life.

Never forget: you embodied love before the traumatic

experiences that taught you fear. Love is your true nature. Fear is what you learned to believe.

How to Choose Love over Fear

To choose love over fear is to return to your natural state of wholeness. Fear contracts; love expands. Fear builds walls; love opens doors. Choosing love is not a single act but a daily practice, a conscious decision to respond with compassion instead of control, curiosity instead of judgment, and trust instead of doubt. When you meet life's challenges through the lens of love, you no longer seek safety in certainty but in self-awareness. Love becomes both your compass and your guide, leading you back to peace, power, and truth.

Reflect

Shifting from fear to love is not a one-time decision but a daily devotion to healing, choosing, and returning home to who you really are.

- Fear often hides in plain sight, disguised as control, anxiety, avoidance, or self-doubt. The first step is bringing it into the light.
- Identify the fears currently driving your choices. Are you acting from love, or protecting yourself from loss, rejection, or failure?
- What fears are in charge of your life right now? Where did they begin? What younger part of you is still fearful and still trying to stay safe?
- Reflect on your emotional memory. When was the last time fear influenced your feelings? How did that affect the outcome?

Journaling Prompt: *What fears are running the show right now and when did they begin? What younger part of me is still trying to stay safe or play small?*

Reframe

Fear is loud, but love is wise. You don't have to silence fear, you just have to stop letting it lead.

- Fear is not your identity; it's a protective belief system built from past pain. It served you once, but you've outgrown it.
- Choosing love doesn't mean you'll never feel afraid again. It means choosing trust, presence and compassion over fear.
- Even small acts of love toward yourself, others, or the world can interrupt fear and rewire your nervous system toward safety and peace.

Mantra: *Fear may visit, but love leads. When I feel fear, I am safe to choose love again.*

Reconnect

Returning to love is a practice, one of remembering, re-centering, and reparenting the parts of you that learned fear too early.

- See beauty first. Wear rose-colored glasses not to deny reality, but to train your mind to look for love before fear.
- Hand over your fear. You don't have to carry it anymore. Offer it to God, the universe, or your higher self and breathe.

- When in doubt, consult your inner child. Ask: "What would I tell my six-year-old self right now?" Then act on the most loving answer.

Affirmation: *I am no longer led by fear. I trust the voice of love within me to guide me, to protect me, and to restore me.*

Final Thought: Love Is the Bravest Thing You Can Do

Choosing love isn't always easy.
It doesn't mean pretending fear doesn't exist.
It means meeting your fear, with open eyes,
a steady heart, and a deeper truth.

Love is not weakness.
Love is strength in its purest form, the kind that says:

I will not abandon myself anymore.
I will not stay small for someone else's comfort.
I will not let fear dictate how my story unfolds.

Every moment gives you a choice.
Every breath is a chance to return to love, for yourself, for your life, for the path ahead.

Let that be the revolution.
Let that be your new default.
Let love lead, always.

Fear is not your destiny.
Love is.
Love is the original language.
The true compass.
The Sovereign choice.

This is Sovereign Living.

HEAD TO HEART

"Broadly speaking, you must follow your instincts, your gut, your first reaction. Your heart is the gateway to your intuition. When you listen to your heart, you can stand in your honor."
~ Gregg Braden

Have you ever second-guessed a decision when you were torn between what makes logical sense and what simply feels right?

That's the classic tug-of-war between head and heart. The mind calculates risk. The heart feels the truth. Both are powerful. But Sovereignty often requires knowing when to quiet the head and surrender to the heart, where the soul speaks without fear.

Science has shown that the heart contains as many sensory neurons as the brain. Your heart is a source of emotion, intuition, and embodied knowing. So the question isn't whether to trust the heart. It's when.

Rely on your mind for planning and strategy, especially in business. But when it comes to relationships, healing, and crucial choices in life, the heart always knows. And the heart, like any muscle, strengthens with use. It grows wiser through joy and deeper through heartbreak.

My Story: I Lost Them in Fear, I Reached for Them in Love

My two eldest children were so hurt by my decision to leave their father that they cut ties with me and my entire family. I was not invited to their proms, graduations, and the first wedding. They had heard about an emotional connection I formed outside the marriage, and without the full context, it was difficult for them to understand my choices. In their uncertainty, they stepped back to find steadiness in a moment that felt overwhelming and unfamiliar. I knew in my heart their distance came from confusion, not a loss of love.

While a part of me trusted that time would eventually bring clarity, I lived with that ache every day. It was the cost of choosing a path I believed was necessary for my own wellbeing and for the greater harmony of our lives. Thankfully, my youngest daughter chose to stand by me.

Ten years after my divorce, came another loss, my father. And with it, a brief text message from my son Max: "Maddie told me about grandpa this morning. I'm really sorry and I hope everyone is doing alright."

I froze. My breath caught. The grief, the gratitude, the divine timing all landed at once. I had lost my brother. Then, emotionally, I lost my son. And now my father. But here was Max, a grown man now, reaching out.

I replied: "Thank you, Max. I let Papa know how much you loved him, and I know how much he loved you."

What I really wanted was to invite Max to come to his grandfather's funeral, but the impulse was met with fear: fear of rejection and fear of placing him in a position where he might have to say no after already finding the courage to reach out. It felt as though asking him to come would be asking for more than he was ready to give.

After my father's funeral, I returned home to regroup, to rest, and to make sense of the sudden loss of my father and the unexpected outreach from my son. In my heart, it felt as though my father had somehow nudged Max forward, passing along a quiet invitation for him to step into the space he left behind.

Back in LA, I tried to process it all. My dear friend CC invited me for a beach walk, and as I shared the story, she suddenly interrupted me.

"What the f'ck, Laura? You didn't go see your son? What's wrong with you?"

She wasn't judging me. She was speaking from her own pain. She was a woman who lost both parents when she was young.

"Why can't the adults be the f'ckn adults?" she said. "Be an adult. Text him. Now."

And I did.

My message to Max:

"Hi Max, I just left you a voicemail. I was trying to say that I miss you and love you and would like the chance to start over again. You and your sisters are the most important family to me, but you and I do not have a relationship. I never thought in a million years the choice I made over 10 years ago would place a wedge between us. I would have chosen 100% differently. All we have is family and the unconditional love that comes with it. I surrender. Let's start again. One phone call to start. I love you. ♥"

That message changed everything. When ego quiets, the heart speaks with vulnerability, honesty, and deep love. And when we meet others in that sacred space, healing becomes possible.

Today Max and I have a fully restored and beautiful relationship. We've had truly precious moments, including his wedding weekend, the birth of his first son, holidays and birthdays. We regularly share texts and weekly phone calls. The bonus to all of this is the respectful and loving relationship I share with his wife Laura, and her parents.

My heart is fuller than I ever imagined it could be.

How to Tap into Your Heart Before Your Ego

The ego wants to protect, defend, and control. The heart wants to connect, heal, and expand. In moments of tension, distance, or indecision, the key is not to silence the ego, but to let the heart speak first. This practice helps you soften, listen inward, and lead with love.

Reflect

Begin by noticing when your mind has been louder than your heart, and how that has shaped your choices.

- Is there someone you love but have distanced yourself from because of pride, fear, or self-protection?
- Where in your life are you stuck in your head, overthinking, overanalyzing, or second-guessing?
- Recall a moment when you ignored your intuition. What was the cost?

Journaling Prompt: *Where have I let ego lead instead of my heart? What would shift if I allowed my heart to go first, even if it feels vulnerable?*

Reframe

Your heart is deeply wise. Choosing your heart doesn't mean erasing boundaries; it means aligning with your deeper truth.

- Reaching out doesn't erase what happened, but it creates space for a new future to emerge.
- The ego seeks control, but the heart seeks truth and healing.
- Vulnerability is not a weakness. It's the bravest doorway to authentic connection.

Mantra: *My heart knows the way; fear steps aside. My boundaries protect my truth, not my walls. Each act of vulnerability opens the way for healing, connection, and a future built on love.*

Reconnect

Connection begins with a softening, a willingness to return to love, even if you were once hurt. Let your healing ripple outward.

- What would love do right now, if it were leading this moment?
- If there's a relationship in need of repair, take one gentle step: a message, a call, or an honest conversation.
- Soften. Speak from your heart, not your wounds. Let the other person feel seen, not judged.
- During my own healing, I practiced the *Sopurkh* mantra, a sacred chant for divine masculine healing. I visualized my son, my brother and my

father. The sound softened my heart and restored peace from within.

Affirmation: *I lead with love, not fear. My heart is my guide, my strength, and my home.*

Final Thought: Let the Heart Take the Lead

The head plans the safest path.
The ego guards old stories tightly.
The heart leads you toward truth.
The heart carries you home.

You don't need perfect language.
You don't need promised outcomes.
You only need inner courage.
Take one brave, honest step.

Move with your heart's clear rhythm.
Speak with your heart's soft power.
Live with your heart's deep meaning.
Let your heart be your compass.

Let your mind serve gently.
Let old control dissolve.
What matters is how you love.
What matters is how you live.

This is Sovereign Living.

SEPARATION TO ONE

*"We are all one.
Only egos, beliefs and
fears separate us."*
~ *Nikola Tesla*

Whether you believe in God, quantum physics, dark energy, the Big Bang, or the essence of Namaste, a single truth remains: We all come from one source.

Science and spirituality use different languages, but both affirm our connection. We are not separate. We are One.

What Does It Mean to Be ONE?

It means that part of you exists in every other life, in the tree outside your window, in your neighbor, in the stranger on the sidewalk. The boundaries between us are not as solid as they seem.

So the question becomes: "How will you choose to show up for yourself and for others?"

The answer doesn't require grand gestures. It begins with compassion. With awareness. With a simple choice to see that what is sacred in yourself is sacred in others.

As children, we did this naturally. If someone fell, we helped them up. If someone had less, we shared.

Then somewhere along the way, we were taught to fend for ourselves. Helping others became inconvenient, uncomfortable, and even unsafe.

But Sovereignty isn't "what's in it for me." Sovereignty isn't isolation. It's the freedom to choose love in action.

My Story: Choosing Love in a World of Disconnection

I live in a place of contrast, the seaside city of Malibu. There's extreme wealth. There are also people sleeping on the beach, in parked cars, and in tents in the hills.

Many see this disparity as someone else's problem. But I can't unsee what I've lived.

My brother struggled with mental illness and addiction. He owned a home but sometimes he chose to live on the streets. As a new mother, I often woke to find him asleep on my porch. I'd step over him gently, a baby balanced on my hip, a briefcase clutched in my hand, hurrying toward my cousin Connie's house, where she cared tenderly for my little one, enabling me to go to work.

I felt like I was failing in both my roles, as a mother and a sister. I was torn between trying to begin one life and saving another.

Now, when I see unhoused men outside my office rummaging and hollow-eyed, I see my brother. And I ask myself: *What would love do?*

Doing nothing wasn't an option. So I joined a group of women who cook and serve meals to the unhoused. As a realtor I may not be able to offer them a house, but I can offer a taste of home. No judgment. Just nourishment. Just care.

Some people in our community criticize the effort, believing it attracts more homelessness. But the homeless are already here. We can ignore them, fear them, blame them.

Or we can see them. Separation is often invisible, built through small judgments, conditioned fears, or a sense of "us versus them." But when we remember that we belong to one another, walls come down. This practice invites you to shift from division to unity, from protection to presence.

Though I am unable to solve homelessness or addiction, I choose to engage with people who have been separated from society, their families, and even from themselves.

That's disconnection, and that's why reconnecting matters.

How to Connect as ONE from Separation

Separation is often invisible, built through small judgments, conditioned fears, or a sense of "us versus them." But when we remember that we belong to one another, walls soften. Connection doesn't require agreement; it requires humanity. This practice invites you to shift from division to unity, from protection to presence.

Reflect

Connection begins with awareness. Where have you built walls instead of bridges, intentionally or unconsciously?

- Reflect on people or groups you may have "othered" based on behavior, beliefs, or background. What stories did you create about them?

- Where do you notice separation showing up in your world, in your community, your relationships, or even your thoughts?

- Recall a time when someone extended compassion or understanding toward you when you didn't expect it. What impact did that have?

Journaling Prompt: *Where have I created distance when I could have offered curiosity or compassion? How might I begin to see others, especially those I struggle with, as part of the same human family?*

Reframe

When we remember that every person carries a story, compassion becomes natural. Separation loses power when we choose to see with the heart.

- The unhoused person is not a statistic. He or she is someone's child, someone's story.

- A difficult co-worker may be fighting battles you can't see. You don't need to fix everyone, but recognize their humanity.

- People you disagree with aren't your enemy. They are on a different path. They are not a different worth.

Mantra: *I release the illusion of separation. I choose to see others as part of me, worthy, whole, and human.*

Reconnect

Bridge the gap with small, intentional acts of kindness. Love isn't loud; it's consistent, compassionate, and creative.

- Perform one quiet act of kindness today. Not for recognition, but as a gesture of unity. Let it ripple.
- Leave behind something uplifting: a note, a book, a compliment, or a care package. Let someone feel seen.
- Reach out to someone grieving, struggling, or overlooked. A simple, sincere message can remind them: *You're not alone.*

Affirmation: *I am connected to every soul I meet. My kindness is a thread that weaves the world back together.*

Final Thought: Remember Who You Are

You are not separate.
You never were.
The moment you choose to see another,
truly see them, you remember the part of yourself
that forgot it was whole.

Oneness isn't a spiritual concept.
It's a daily practice.
It lives in your eyes when you meet a stranger's gaze.
It breathes in your actions when you extend
compassion instead of critique.

There will always be reasons to divide:
beliefs, politics, class, pain.
But love finds its way through all of it.
One kind gesture. One conscious moment.
One choice to connect instead of reject.

So today, choose the radical act of remembering:
You belong. They belong.
That's where unity begins.
That's when healing happens.

This is Sovereign Living.

SERVE OTHERS TO SERVING SELF, FIRST

"In case of a cabin pressure emergency, put on your own mask first before assisting others."
~ Every airline flight attendant, every flight

You've probably heard that safety instruction dozens of times before takeoff. But how often do we apply it to our everyday lives?

We give and give and give to our children, our partners, our coworkers, and our communities, until we're depleted. And then we wonder why we feel tired, resentful, or uninspired.

Here's the truth: you can't share water from an empty well. Sovereignty begins by filling your own cup first, so that everything you give comes from overflow, not obligation.

Imagine a version of your life where you're energized, grounded, and deeply present. Where your joy fuels your relationships, your clarity sharpens your purpose, and your self-love becomes a ripple effect of healing for those around you.

If this sounds good, raise your hand! Now raise it again if you know your family, workplace, or community would benefit from that version of you.

My Story: From Self-Abandonment to Self-Honor

For years, I lived by this inaccurate equation: Sacrifice = Love.

I placed everyone else's needs above my own. I kept doing it, until I couldn't.

That realization came to me during a job interview. A prospective employer looked at my resume and asked, "Are you really living in Redding?"

I was living in Redding, CT. A quiet New England town with two-acre zoning, no sidewalks, no grocery store or movie theater. A great place to raise kids, but isolating if you're someone, like myself, who craves creative energy, diversity, and modern conveniences.

He said, gently, "I just don't see you living there."

I froze. Then words tumbled out: "I was living someone else's dream."

That moment was an epiphany. I had shapeshifted into a version of myself that mirrored my husband's vision of a good life, losing sight of my own along the way.

When I shared my desire to move, my words seemed to drift past unheard, and in that silence, I convinced myself to stay. It seems almost ironic that I tried to adjust by buying a bigger house in the same town. Would more space create more happiness? It didn't.

When you don't meet your own needs, everyone pays the price. Especially the people you were trying so hard to protect.

I look back now with heartfelt gratitude. We were fortunate to raise our children in a beautiful, safe community with a highly rated school district, even though as a working mother I had hoped to live in a location that better supported our daily life.

How Do We Nourish Ourselves Before Others?

It starts by listening to yourself, not just to others. It means remembering that your dreams matter. That your needs are valid. You're not only in service to others' needs. You're in service to your own.

Nourishing yourself isn't a retreat from love, it's a return to it. When you meet your own needs with compassion and intention, you can show up for others with authenticity, energy, and grace. Self-nourishment is the root of sustainable giving.

Reflect

Before you can refill your cup, you must see where it's leaking:

- Have you been living to meet others' expectations, while your own desires sit quietly in the background?
- What part of your life feels overextended or ignored, your body, your spirit, your time, your dreams?
- When was the last time you said "yes" out of obligation, even though your body or heart was saying "no"?

Journaling Prompt: *Where in my life am I abandoning my own needs in order to meet someone else's? What would it look like to turn some of that care inward, starting today?*

Reframe

Self-prioritization is not a betrayal of love; it's the foundation of it. You lead with greater impact when you're rooted in self-awareness.

- Self-care is not self-indulgent. It's essential. You are the vessel through which your love flows.
- Putting yourself first doesn't mean putting others last. You give from overflow, not from depletion.
- Your needs are not inconveniences. They are sacred signals pointing you toward alignment and purpose.
- Nourishing yourself is an act of love for all.

Mantra: *When I honor my needs, I honor my purpose. Nourishing myself is an act of love for all.*

Reconnect

Once you've reclaimed your right to receive, rebuild your life around self-nourishment, not as a luxury but as a daily rhythm.

- Ask yourself what you truly desire, not just what's expected of you. Write it down.
- Create a visual reminder of this desire: a vision board, a sketch, a sticky note. Let it live in your space.
- Identify a few small steps that move you toward this desire. Take one step today.

Affirmation: *I deserve to be well, whole, and fully alive. When I care for myself, I rise in service to others from a place of truth and strength.*

Final Thought: Self-Sacrifice Is Not a Superpower

Martyrdom is not a measure of love.
Exhaustion is not a badge of honor.
Your worth is not defined by how much you endure.
It is defined by how fully you show up as yourself.

Choosing yourself first is not abandonment.
It is alignment.
It is choosing wholeness over depletion.
It is giving from overflow rather than obligation.

When you nourish yourself,
your life becomes the lesson.
Your presence becomes the teaching.
Your energy becomes the gift.
Your joy becomes the service.

You are not here to disappear into the needs of others.
You are here to be fully alive.
You are here to be fully expressed.

This is the new model of service.
And it starts with you.

This is Sovereign Living.

HOLDING GUILT & SHAME TO BECOMING VULNERABLE

> *"Shame is the intensely painful feeling or experience of believing that we are flawed and therefore unworthy of love and belonging. Shame means, 'I am bad.' Guilt means, 'I did something bad.'"*
>
> *"When we want greater clarity in our purpose or deeper and more meaningful spiritual lives, vulnerability is the path."*
>
> ~ Brené Brown

We are born whole, open-hearted, vulnerable, and full of love. Then guilt arises when we believe we have done something wrong. Shame goes deeper, convincing us that, beyond doing something wrong, we are something wrong. Over time, these quiet emotions shape how we show up in life, in love, and in our own sense of worth.

When we carry those wounds into adulthood, into partnership, parenting, or even friendship, they begin to color how we connect and communicate. Misunderstandings grow, distance widens, and unspoken resentment can quietly take hold. Sometimes it leads to separation or divorce, experiences that can stir deep guilt and shame. Yet even in those endings lies an invitation to see not failure, but transformation. Divorce, when met with compassion, can become a passage back to truth, healing, and the rediscovery of love in its most honest form.

Reframing Divorce

Divorce has long been cast in the shadows as something to be ashamed of and kept quiet. But what if we viewed it differently?

Divorce isn't a failure. It can be freedom, a courageous act of re-alignment, a decision to stop performing and start living with truth. It doesn't define you. It refines you. It's part of your evolution, not your identity.

Emotional intelligence and vulnerability are essential in any relationship, especially the one you have with yourself. A healthy relationship requires two whole people, not two shape-shifted versions trying to live up to each other's projections.

My Story: The Cost of Being Everything to Everyone but Myself

I didn't understand how guilt and shame shaped me until long after my divorce. While married, I tried to be the perfect version of everything: mother, homemaker, school and community volunteer, cheerleading coach, professional and host for holiday gatherings. I chased perfection with relentless energy. If I just did more, I'd be more lovable. But I never rested. I never paused. I never asked myself what I truly needed.

There was guilt for not being a stay-at-home mom, and equal guilt from co-workers when I left early for family needs. The irony? I always made it work: family cared for, deadlines met, everything done.

Yet I still felt like I was letting everyone down. The person I actually let down was myself.

Practices for Releasing Guilt and Shame and Embracing Vulnerability

Guilt and shame are powerful emotions, often rooted in the past but quietly influencing the present. Vulnerability is not weakness. It's the sacred doorway to healing, connection, and freedom.

These practices are meant to help you soften self-judgment, reclaim compassion, and reconnect with your whole self.

Reflect

To release guilt or shame, you must first acknowledge where it lives emotionally, physically, and energetically.

- Recall a specific moment that left you with lingering guilt or shame. What happened, and how did you respond?
- Where did you feel it in your body? Did it show up as tightness, heat, heaviness, or something else?
- Does that moment still carry emotional weight today? If so, what story are you still holding onto?

Journaling Prompt: *What experience still carries guilt or shame in your body? How has it shaped your self-perception? Are you ready to release that experience?*

Reframe

Reframing invites compassion to step in and re-tell your story with love and clarity.

- Are you revisiting the past with harsh judgment or with the same grace you would offer someone you love?

- Can you offer empathy not only to yourself, but also to others involved in the moment? Everyone was learning.

- What if that moment wasn't a failure, but a necessary part of your becoming?

Insight Practice: *What would shift if I viewed this not as a wound to punish, but as a lesson to love myself through?*

Reconnect

Vulnerability is the pathway back to wholeness. True healing happens when you stop hiding your heart from yourself or others.

- What would it look like to be more emotionally honest with yourself, or with someone tied to that pain?

- Express your feelings, not to control their reaction, but to free your own truth. This is *your* release.

- Begin a forgiveness practice like Ho'oponopono, a traditional Hawaiian practice of reconciliation and forgiveness: *"I'm sorry. Please forgive me. Thank you. I love you."* Speak the words slowly. Let the emotion move through you. Try reciting this daily for 40 days. Use rosary or mala beads to guide repetition and deepen healing.

Affirmation: *I release the weight of shame. I forgive myself and others with compassion. I am free to heal, to feel, and to begin again.*

Final Thought: The Truth Will Set You Free, But First It May Break You Open

Guilt and shame keep us small.
They trap us in old cycles.
Perfection becomes a quiet cage.
Vulnerability is the key.

To live Sovereignly is to live truthfully.
It means speaking your heart.
It means saying "This hurt me."
And saying "I made a mistake."

It means saying "I'll try again."
It means holding your wounds gently.
It means forgiving yourself often.
Your worth is your willingness to be seen.

To be human is to be flawed.
To be Sovereign is to stay loving.
Let the old shame fall away.

This is not your undoing.
This is your becoming.

This is Sovereign Living.

ADDICTION TO AWARENESS

"This is the age of addiction, a condition so epidemic, so all-encompassing that you may not even know if you have it."
~ Russell Brand

We often associate addiction with substances, alcohol, drugs, or gambling, but addiction can be far more subtle. It can hide in everyday habits, emotional patterns, and unconscious needs. Those kinds of addictions often stem from unmet emotional needs or inherited behaviors that go unexamined.

How does a child grow into an adult with addictive patterns? Often we blame genetics: "It runs in the family." But as adults, especially parents, we may model addictive choices, whether consciously or not. Children are always watching, learning not just from what we say, but what we do. If we numb ourselves with alcohol, overwork, or other addictive behaviors, they see all of that.

My Story: Love Looked Like Approval, Until I Finally Saw the Difference

I grew up in a household shadowed by substance abuse. That experience shaped my early commitment to avoid the same path. I felt proud to be free from it. I saw myself as someone on the "clean side" of the destruction, not causing it, but managing the aftermath.

One evening I discovered the truth, and I didn't see it coming.

A dear friend, lovingly nicknamed Monkey, invited me to a last-minute charity event supporting those affected by Hurricane Harvey in Houston. One of my children was living there then, and the city pressed gently on my heart. Showing up that night became a way to channel my love into action, to meet uncertainty with compassion, and to join my Malibu community in lifting others during a moment of profound need.

The event was casual, "BYOB." I brought a bottle of wine. Not long into the evening, a man approached me and asked, "So what's your addiction?"

Caught off guard, I assumed it was a clumsy attempt at flirtation. He added that most of the evening's attendees had met through AA. I looked down at my wine and said, "I'm addicted to appreciation."

He laughed. "That's not an addiction."

But suddenly I knew that's exactly what it was.

I was addicted to feeling seen, acknowledged, and appreciated. I realized I had come to rely on external validation in order to feel worthy. A simple "thank you" or recognition of my effort felt essential. If it didn't come, I felt hurt, invisible, unimportant.

Raised as the firstborn by a mother who praised me for being helpful and accomplished, I equated love with approval. Appreciation and admiration became my fuel.

This awareness shook me. It also freed me. From that point on, I began to ask myself, *"No matter what I'm doing, is it with a full heart? Am I doing it for me, or for someone else's approval?"*

When I share love, like in volunteering, it fills me up, whether I'm acknowledged or not. But when I give, hoping for a response and don't receive one, I feel depleted.

It wasn't until I dated someone who shared my same emotional addiction that I finally saw myself with full understanding. He was generous, attentive to detail and often anticipated my needs before I voiced them. But if I didn't show appreciation, especially for things I hadn't asked for, he grew frustrated.

I realized I had sometimes done the same thing. If I offered unsolicited help, I felt angry or disappointed if it wasn't appreciated. I wasn't giving freely. I was giving with strings, invisible but tangled in expectation.

I began to understand how relationships, personal or professional, require clarity, reciprocity, and honest communication. Otherwise we're just reenacting our unmet needs through other people.

These patterns often begin as survival mechanisms. Healing them requires self-awareness, gentle reprogramming, and a return to internal stability.

How to Cultivate Awareness and Heal Emotional Addiction

Emotional addiction isn't just about substances or behaviors; it's about patterns we cling to in order to feel loved, worthy, or safe. Whether it's the need to be needed, praised, or in control, these patterns often begin as survival mechanisms. Healing them requires self-awareness, gentle reprogramming, and a return to internal stability.

Reflect

Awareness is the first act of healing. By tracing your emotional patterns back to their roots, you begin to reclaim your power.

- Where in your life do you consistently feel unseen, unappreciated, or emotionally depleted?
- Can you name behaviors that feel compulsive, like over-giving, people-pleasing, or needing constant validation?
- What beliefs were modeled for you about what earns love, praise, or a sense of worth? Who taught you those lessons?

Journaling Prompt: *When did you first begin seeking external validation, and from whom? Has that shaped how you seek to "prove your value" today?*

Reframe

When emotional addiction is a response to early unmet needs, reframing helps to release shame and step into empowered choice.

- Emotional patterns that once protected you may now be limiting your growth, they were tools, not truths.
- Ask yourself honestly: "What am I gaining by repeating this cycle?" "What am I losing by staying in it?"
- Appreciation feels good, but it's not evidence of your worth. You are inherently valuable, even when unseen.

Empowering Question: *What if I gave from fullness instead of fear? How would it feel to be free from needing a response to feel enough?*

Reconnect

Healing emotional addiction means reconnecting to your own internal source of value, and modeling what it means to love yourself first.

- Identify one emotional addiction. Track where and how it appears in your relationships and routines.

- Observe your emotional responses when others don't meet your expectations. Don't judge, just gather insight and compassion for yourself.

- Support your healing with therapy, coaching, or resources like podcasts, books, or trusted communities. You don't have to do it alone.

Affirmation: *I am no longer ruled by the need to be validated. I value myself fully and I give from love, not lack.*

Final Thought: From Craving to Clarity

Addiction is a longing.
It is a search for what feels missing.
What we seek outside is a reflection.
It mirrors what we're learning to give ourselves.

Awareness doesn't ask for perfection.
It asks you to pause.
It asks you to notice.
It asks you to listen within.

"Is this what I need?"
"Or is this an old echo?"
These questions soften the craving.
They bring you back to yourself.

You fill your cup with truth.
You choose with clarity.
You give from overflow.
You reclaim your power.

This is Sovereign Living.

CONDITIONAL TO UNCONDITIONAL LOVE

> *"Unconditional love is a journey of self-discovery, where we learn to love ourselves fully and extend that love to others."*
>
> ~ *Osho*

Unconditional love is often misunderstood. It's not just the warm, fuzzy feeling we associate with "being in love." True unconditional love means fully accepting another person just as they are, even when they don't meet our expectations or reflect our beliefs.

It means loving someone even when they're "wrong" in your eyes, even when they make choices that challenge you. That kind of love doesn't flinch. It holds steady without controlling and without conditions.

It starts with how we love ourselves.

My Story: Learning to Love Myself As I've Always Loved Others

I grew up knowing what unconditional love felt like. My mother gave it freely to me, my sister, and my brother. No matter how much we pushed, tested, or acted out, her love remained steady, quiet, and fierce. She loved us all through everything, often without taking care of herself.

I know I've extended that same unconditional love to my children, even when I felt rejected after my divorce. Even when they pulled away, I never stopped loving them. That's how I know unconditional love is possible.

I've also loved my parents unconditionally. As a teen, I questioned my father's love. But as an adult, I saw how he showed love in his own quiet, unwavering way. I trusted that my parents were always doing their best, and that built the foundation of deep, abiding love.

I've struggled most in romantic relationships. Looking back, I see that I hadn't yet learned to love myself unconditionally, so I attracted men who also lacked that inner self-love. We mirrored each other's limitations.

Once I saw this clearly, I began turning inward. I pulled out a metaphorical flashlight and examined the places where I still judged myself, where I was doing things to gain approval rather than acting from authenticity. I started saying no to what didn't align. I began prioritizing my needs, then accommodating others only from a full cup, not from obligation.

I surrounded myself with people who matched my energy. I gave love to those who truly saw me. And in return I received deep, unconditional love, especially from my children.

I restructured my days to put God first, then myself, then others. I cleared time each morning to write this book, not just as a legacy, but as an act of love for my future self, my children, and their children. Writing became an offering, a sacred routine. Some days it felt like my life depended on it.

I reexamined my work relationships and chose to invest my energy only in clients who genuinely value my expertise. I claimed clarity around the income required for a life of abundance, freedom, and spontaneous joy. I even created a budget line for "unexpected joy," because true love includes tending to your own delight, whether that means a spa day, new tires, or a last-minute getaway.

I became intentional about how I show up in my relationships with my children as they move through their own adult lives. I choose my words and actions with care, offering support that honors who they are now as partners, parents, business professionals, and evolving humans. I value the time we share, the love we exchange, and the mutual respect we continue to build.

To stay grounded and healthy, I've committed to a daily practice of meditation, yoga, light strength training, mostly clean eating, hydration, and 5,000+ steps a day. I go to the beach at least three times a week. I limit TV. I only check social media at night. I've even come to appreciate my aging skin as lines of wisdom, evidence of a life well lived.

And the more I give to myself, time, presence, and compassion, the more I feel *in love* with myself, and in love with the people around me.

How to Cultivate Unconditional Self-Love

Unconditional self-love isn't about ignoring flaws. It's about embracing the whole of who you are, even as you grow. It's choosing compassion over critique, presence over performance, and worthiness over waiting. This practice helps you return home to yourself, again and again, with softness, truth, and grace.

Reflect

True self-love begins with honest self-inquiry. You can't fully love yourself until you see the places where love has been withheld.

- Have you done the work to love yourself completely, not just in your strengths, but in your messiness, mistakes, and humanity?
- Who in your life do you love unconditionally? What makes it easy (or hard) to do so?
- Are there places where you're still chasing love through perfection, approval, or productivity?

Journaling Prompt: *Where in my life is my self-love still conditional? What would it look like to love myself without needing to be "better" first?*

Reframe

Self-love is a daily practice you choose. When you stop outsourcing love, you start reclaiming your power.

- Unconditional love must begin with the self. No one else can give you what you're unwilling to offer yourself.

- Conditional self-love often hides in phrases like "I'll love myself when…" Or, "Once I achieve this, then I'll rest." What if right now is enough?

- Loving yourself in the "messy middle" is radical. It's a declaration: I am worthy here, too.

Empowering Question: *What would shift if I chose to love myself, not later, but now, as I am?*

Reconnect

Unconditional self-love becomes real through how you speak to yourself, care for yourself, and honor your needs daily.

- Make a list of small ways to show yourself love today: saying no without apology, speaking gently to yourself, resting without guilt.

- Set boundaries with those who deplete you, even if you care about them. Your energy matters.

- Practice receiving love from others without deflection or downplaying. Let love land. Let it nourish you.

Affirmation: *I am worthy of love without conditions. I choose to love, protect, and honor myself fully, freely, and now.*

Final Thought: Love Without Conditions Begins With You

Unconditional love is not a lofty ideal.
It is a daily practice.
It is choosing presence over performance.
It is choosing truth over perfection.

It is choosing compassion over control.
It does not require staying in harm.
It does not excuse unhealthy dynamics.
It invites clear seeing, with grace.

It means loving flaws and humanity.
It means holding boundaries with care.
It means meeting yourself with tenderness.
It means offering love from overflow.

This is the power of unconditional love.
As you remember, you return to it.
You become a steady source of it.
You don't earn love. You remember it.

That is Sovereign Living.

PROJECTING TO PROTECTING

"Don't take anything personally. Nothing others do is because of you. What others say and do is a projection of their own reality, their own dream. When you are immune to the opinions and actions of others, you won't be the victim of needless suffering."
~ Don Miguel Ruiz

Projection is a psychological mechanism for transferring your own fears, wounds, or desires onto someone else. It's usually an unconscious process, but it can also be done on purpose. Often we use projection in the name of love, especially with our children, thinking we're helping or protecting.

In other words, you may mean well, but...

My Story: She Already Knew and I Just Had to Get Out of the Way

When my youngest daughter was approaching college graduation, she felt an overwhelming pressure to make every major life decision all at once. She was navigating her final semester, aiming for straight A's in order to graduate magna cum laude. She was also contemplating whether to live and look for a job in New York or in Los Angeles.

Factored into that decision was a long-term boyfriend who was based in her university town and deeply rooted in his family's business. She also had a tight-knit group of college girlfriends who shared a deep desire to squeeze in all the bucket-list experiences they had dreamed about freshman year, before they scattered across the country. Her heart was full. So was her plate.

During her holiday visit home, she and I sat down to sort through the options. LA or NY? Boyfriend or new adventure? College girlfriends or new connections? I offered what I thought was solid advice, a blend of practicality and maternal wisdom. My daughter seemed relieved, even grateful. We hugged and said goodnight.

But I didn't sleep well. By morning I realized I had unintentionally projected my own life experiences onto my daughter. I had repeated advice given to me by my mother 30 years earlier. That was advice from a very different experience, time and setting.

I rushed to correct myself. Over coffee that Christmas morning, I explained that I might have misstepped. The advice I gave may not apply to her life at all, and that I wanted to take it back.

She gave me a puzzled look. "So now what do you think I should do?"

Instead of answering, I asked her some real questions:

- *What do you want?*
- *Does your life now fulfill you or drain you?*
- *What future do you see for yourself?*
- *Are you giving what you want to give, or what you want to receive?*
- *Is your energy being reciprocated?*

Only she could answer those. And she did, over time.

She stayed in the relationship with her boyfriend for another year, long-distance. Eventually, she chose to end it for reasons she had already sensed.

After graduation, she moved to LA, explored job opportunities, then shifted back to NY for more interviews. Finally she landed a dream job in LA just blocks from where we were living. Her friendships have remained strong. She now lives minutes from two of her best college friends and has been in a healthy, loving relationship for over five years with a partner who grew up in LA.

How to Support Without Projecting

True support is not about fixing, rescuing, or redirecting. It's about creating space for someone to access their own wisdom, in their own time. When we release the need to project our past onto someone else's present, we offer the powerful gift of presence, not prescription.

Reflect

Before offering guidance, pause to examine your motivation. Self-awareness helps you give support from a place of clarity rather than assumption.

- Reflect on a time you gave advice based more on *your* experience than the other person's reality. What was driving you?
- Have you ever regretted offering guidance that didn't land or wasn't truly aligned with their needs?
- Consider moments when your urge to protect may have disrupted someone else's opportunity to grow, stumble, or decide for themselves.

Journaling Prompt: *When have I offered support from a place of fear, memory, or control? How might I shift toward curiosity and trust instead?*

Reframe

Let go of the belief that love must look like intervention. Empowerment often looks like stepping back.

- Supporting someone doesn't mean directing their path; it means believing in their ability to find it.
- Your lived experience is valuable, but it's not the universal truth. Their story may unfold differently and beautifully.

- Asking thoughtful, reflective questions creates space for insight. It's often more helpful than offering pre-packaged advice.

Empowering Question: *What if the most loving thing I can offer is not my answer but my trust in their own?*

Reconnect

Choose presence over projection. Hold space for someone else's process with humility, warmth, and restraint.

- When someone seeks your guidance, pause. Listen first. Then ask questions that draw out their own clarity: "What do you feel drawn to?" "What are you afraid of?" "What choice brings peace to your body, not just your mind?"

- Be aware of your tone and energy. Curiosity fosters openness. Certainty can raise defenses.

- If you recognize what you've projected, acknowledge it with grace. Reconnect through honesty: "I realize I made this about me. Thank you for your patience."

Affirmation: *I support with presence, not pressure. I trust your journey. I honor your timing. I let love listen.*

Final Thought: From Guiding to Holding Space

Love is not fixing.
Love helps others hear themselves.
Advice is not the gift.
Presence is the offering.

Resisting rescue creates strength.
Softening solutions builds trust.
Patience becomes medicine.
Trust becomes guidance.

Your experience is a mirror.
It is not a map.
Reflect possibility, not direction.
Honor their path.

At the crossroads, stay close.
Sit beside them.
Hold the light.
Trust their way.

This is Sovereign Living.

DECISION MAKING FROM THE SUBCONSCIOUS TO FREE WILL

> *"I am an artist, and I have the ability and the free will to choose how the world will envision me."*
>
> ~ *Lady Gaga*

Free will is the conscious power to shape reality for yourself, as well as in the perception of others. But right now, is your life being lived through unconscious programming rather than conscious choice?

Sovereign Living means reclaiming the power to choose, moment by moment, and thought by thought.

The Truth About Decision-Making

Research shows that up to 95% of decisions originate in the subconscious mind, while only about 5% come from the conscious, intentional self.

Why does the subconscious have so much power? If we fear that our choices may conflict with someone else's desires, we may abandon ourselves. We avoid rocking the boat. We delay decisions or hand them off entirely.

This is especially true in close relationships where choices are shared, emotions are entangled, and outcomes are deeply personal. We tell ourselves we're being thoughtful. But often we're avoiding the discomfort of owning our truth.

Free will is not a joint venture. It belongs to you alone. In Sovereign relationships, you must be free to choose, and trust others to do the same.

The Subconscious: Your Silent Scriptwriter

Your subconscious mind is like a massive internal library filled with data, emotions, judgments, values, and experiences you've collected throughout your life. It processes information at lightning speed and can influence decisions before your conscious mind catches up.

This invisible programming can drive how we judge right and wrong, how we respond to risk, and how we define what's possible for us. When left unexamined, the subconscious becomes the default decision-maker. So self-awareness and reprogramming are essential for living with Sovereign intention.

My Story: A "Soulbbatical" in the Homeland

As my 60th birthday approached, I felt a deep and undeniable pull: it was time for a Soulbbatical, a week devoted to soul-searching, daily yoga, nourishing food, and reconnecting with nature. At the same time, I longed to visit Italy, to make a pilgrimage to San Fili, the small village where my father was born and spent his first 18 years before immigrating to the United States.

Two desires, one heart. I wondered, *How could I possibly do both?*

Then, as often happens when we surrender, a quiet voice whispered, *It will happen. Let go of the details.*

Then a newsletter arrived in my inbox from Mandali, a retreat center perched on a hilltop with panoramic views of Lake Orta and the Swiss Alps. It was just an hour drive from Milan. The fall schedule included several options, but one immediately stood out: a Silent Retreat was happening the exact week of my birthday.

Without hesitation I called my dear friend Kimberly and asked, "Will you join me?" Her response was an immediate and joyful: "Yes!" Followed by the more practical, "Wait… can we talk during the Silent Retreat?"

Just like that, my birthday week would be happening in Italy.

Flights were booked and I departed Los Angeles solo for Rome, then onward to Calabria. I took a ferry to Sicily and spent a day wandering Taormina's sun-kissed streets. Each day brought a new town, a new hotel, a new layer of discovery.

In Tropea, I joined a boat excursion and hiked to Santa Maria, a hilltop church. There, I slipped a prayer card into a box, asking God to help reunite me with my eldest daughter. Four months later, she moved from Southeast Texas to Southern California, just a twenty-minute drive from me. There is power in prayers. Trust they are heard.

From Tropea, I flew to Lamezia and rented a little Fiat for the drive to San Fili. Guided by GPS, I arrived at my father's childhood home. I walked the cobblestone streets, taking photos and videos for my family. It was exactly as I had imagined.

I left feeling fulfilled, as if I had completed a sacred act of remembrance. That night, I stayed on the coast in Paola, where my grandparents had spent their summers.

The next morning, I returned the Fiat and flew to Milan, arriving a few days ahead of Kimberly. Another Fiat, another journey, this time to Lake Como. I drove along the water's edge, marveling at the architecture. The best pizza of the entire trip was at Federico's in Cernobbio.

I drove back to the Milan airport to drop off the Fiat and meet Kimberly, who had arrived from NY for our not-so-silent Silent Retreat at Mandali.

The retreat was everything and more, true "la dolce vita." The meals alone were transformative and the people we met from all over the world had come for the same reason as us: to do their inner work.

Our final night was spent back in Milan, where Kimberly surprised me with tickets to the sold-out tour of The Last Supper. Standing before Da Vinci's masterpiece felt like a poetic closing to a deeply meaningful journey, one that honored both my soul and my roots.

Purposeful planning and exercising free will can take you to places far, far away!

How to Reclaim Free Will and Make Conscious Decisions

True freedom begins when you stop living by default and start living by design. Reclaiming your free will means identifying where you've been on autopilot, interrupting fear-based programming, and stepping boldly into self-authored choices. Your life is a sacred creation. You are the one holding the tools.

Reflect

Before you can choose consciously, you must first become aware of where you've been choosing unconsciously.

- Reflect on major life decisions, relationships, careers, lifestyle, that felt more reactive than rooted in your own values.
- Consider moments where you avoided or delayed a decision to maintain someone else's comfort rather than honor your truth.
- Identify where fear, self-doubt, or limiting beliefs may still be steering your actions (e.g., "Don't rock the boat," "Stay small," "Play it safe").

Journaling Prompt: *When have you given away your power by avoiding truth, deferring to others, or operating from fear? What would reclaiming that power look like now?*

Reframe

You're not just a passenger in your life, you're the driver. Reframing helps you take the wheel with clarity, purpose, and self-trust.

- You are the author of your life. Reclaim the pen. Rewrite the script.

- Start with your vision: On your last day, what do you want to have created, contributed, and become? Let that legacy inform today's choices.

- Mistakes are not failures, they're feedback. Every wrong turn helps sharpen your inner compass.

Empowering Question: *If you lived from your desires instead of your fears, what decisions would you make today?*

Reconnect

Free will requires consistent alignment. Anchor into your vision daily and make choices that honor the life you're here to build.

- Make a sacred contract with yourself: no more settling. Write your vision down. Speak it aloud. Let it shape your filters: What stays? What is going? Who expands me? Who drains me?

- Choose your inputs with discernment. Reduce exposure to the noise of polarizing news and negative media. Nourish your spirit with truth, beauty, and possibility.

- Establish grounding practices of meditation, prayer, breathwork, or visualization. Let each morning become a return to your values, your vision, your voice.

Affirmation: *I am a conscious creator. I choose from love, not fear. Each decision is a step toward the life I am meant to live.*

Final Thought: Direct Your Inner Narrative

Your narrative is yours to choose.
Your story begins with awareness.
Your voice shapes your becoming.
Your truth leads you home.

Listen beneath the noise.
Let clarity rise within you.
Let intuition rewrite old scripts.
Let intention guide each step.

You are the author now.
You decide the direction.
You choose the meaning.
You claim the becoming.

Design your life consciously.
Choose from the soul, not fear.
Create what your heart envisions.
Write the story only you can live.

This is Sovereign Living.

AVOIDANCE TO ENGAGEMENT

"Engage your life with enthusiasm, grasp your life aggressively and squeeze from it every drop of excitement, satisfaction and joy."
~ Felix Baumgartner

Why are we here? What are we supposed to be doing with our time on this earth?

These questions can feel overwhelming. But in terms of our shared human experience, the answer is simpler than we think: We are hearts and souls, living in human bodies, trying to feel love, give love, receive love, and belong.

So why do so many people feel disconnected, numb, or shut down? It's fear. Fear of rejection. Fear of inadequacy. Fear of not belonging. Fear born from past pain, a moment that made us afraid of being seen, heard, or open again.

Over time, fear becomes avoidance. We pull away from people, situations, even from ourselves and believe it's safer to stay closed. But disengagement isn't protection. It's isolation. And it's not what we came here for.

Life is for living. Living requires engagement.

My Story: Connection as a Living Cycle

I've always had a natural curiosity about people. I speak to strangers often on planes, in yoga classes, at restaurants. Where are you from? What brought you here? What makes you light up?

My fascination with people has evolved into a gift for connecting, not just in conversation, but in action. I love introducing people to each other. Whether it's for friendship, mentorship, business, or shared experience, I thrive on building bridges and closing gaps.

I've connected strangers in a single text or email who went on to build stronger bonds with each other than I ever had with either of them. And I'm happy about it. That's the beauty of meaningful engagement; it's expansive and generous. You don't lose anything by giving it away. And yet, I also know the importance of stepping back.

When life delivers grief, heartbreak, or a personal setback, I retreat for stillness. I pause to process, to feel the weight of emotion, and to honor what needs to be released. But the withdrawal is temporary. Once healed, I re-engage, fuller, softer, and wiser.

Engagement is not constant output. It's a cycle of opening, connecting, reflecting, and returning.

How to Move from Avoidance to Engagement

Avoidance is often a shield, one that forms in response to fear, rejection, or overwhelm. But connection is a deep human need, and true engagement doesn't require perfection, only presence. When we meet others with curiosity and courage, we begin to dissolve the distance we've built.

Reflect

To engage authentically, you must first understand what's holding you back.

- Where are you currently avoiding connection? Is it in relationships, community, or even with yourself? What lies beneath that hesitation?

- Have past experiences of judgment, rejection, or misunderstanding made you reluctant to reach out?

- Is fear keeping you from being fully seen, heard, or known? Are there people you're drawn to but haven't approached?

- If you assumed people wanted to connect with you, could you act from that truth instead of fear?

Journaling Prompt: *What fears or past experiences are fueling my avoidance? Where am I longing for connection but holding back and why?*

Reframe

Avoidance feels like protection, but it often leads to deeper loneliness. When you reframe connection as a courageous act, you take the first step toward healing.

- Avoidance may feel safe, but it also reinforces the belief that you're not welcome or wanted. That belief is rarely true.

- Most people are waiting for someone to go first. A small gesture can open the door to a meaningful bond.

- You don't need perfect words or timing. Curiosity is enough. Kindness is enough. You are enough!

Empowering Question: *What if I assumed people wanted to connect with me and acted from that truth instead of fear?*

Reconnect

Engagement doesn't require intensity. It begins with presence, consistency, and a willingness to show up imperfectly but authentically.

- Challenge yourself to initiate one genuine connection each day, even if it's as simple as a compliment or a question.
- Revisit someone you've recently met. Reach out. Follow up. Ask about something they shared.
- Spark small conversations using easy prompts:
  – "What's a book or podcast that's inspired you lately?"
  – "What's something small that made you smile today?"
  – "What's one thing you're curious about right now?"

Affirmation: *I am open to connection. I release fear and step into curiosity, knowing that presence is enough.*

Final Thought: Be Brave Enough to Begin Again

The world doesn't need perfect people.
It needs present ones.
It needs lifted eyes.
It needs open hearts.

Every moment is a doorway.
Step back into life.
Say hello.
Ask the question.

Share the smile.
Offer the kindness.
Be sincere, not loud.
Let courage lead you.

Connection heals isolation.
Presence builds community.
Begin again today.
Begin again often.

This is Sovereign Living.

KNOW THY SELF TO KNOWING THY SELF

"Knowing others is intelligence; knowing yourself is true wisdom."
~ Lao Tzu

"There are three extremely hard things: steel, a diamond, and to know oneself."
~ Benjamin Franklin

Stop. Go back. Read "Know Thy Self to Knowing Thy Self" again. Really read it. "Know thy self" is not the same as "Knowing thy self."

The first speaks to external mastery: staying on top of your responsibilities, your work, your business, your beliefs, your commitments.

The second, the deeper one, is self-mastery. Knowing your blind spots, your patterns, your pitfalls, and your unconscious fears that might be keeping you stuck. It's about emotional intelligence. Self-awareness. Vulnerability. Owning your story, even the messy parts.

You should know your stuff, your finances, your profession, your passions, your politics. But do you know yourself? Do you know the behaviors that propel you forward, and more importantly, the ones that hold you back? Do you understand the underlying motivation for how you respond and react?

My Story: Finding the Truth through Others (Blue) Eyes

I'll never forget one second date in particular. He had piercing blue eyes, the kind you remember, and a slight Boston accent.

He looked at me and asked, "So what's your relationship pitfall?"

I thought, *Damn, that's a good question.*

I had never asked myself that question. I mentally scrolled through the key relationships in my life like a highlight reel.

Almost involuntarily, I answered, "I'm incredibly generous with attention and affection. I give all of myself, my time, my energy, my love, in exchange for admiration and appreciation. I become a chameleon. I shapeshift to fit the life of the man I love, believing that treating him like a king will earn me the place of queen. But when appreciation fades, when I no longer feel seen or valued, I grow resentful. I feel depleted. I lose myself. I fall off the throne I built with my own hands."

Yes, that was it. I traded my self-worth for attention. It was one of the most honest things I had ever said out loud in a romantic setting, and it changed me.

I honestly can't recall many details of our brief relationship, but I remember that it ended with respect, gentleness, and mutual understanding. It was a beautiful ending, rooted in awareness. Though short-lived, that relationship remains a meaningful gift in my life.

From that moment on, I made a vow to myself:

I will still love deeply.

I will still be generous.

I will still honor you.

But I will not abandon myself.

There will be no more self-sacrificing.

No more silent suffering.

No more hoping someone reads between the lines.

I will speak clearly. Set boundaries and reinforce them. And always state what I need.

I will show up vulnerably, and expect the same.

I will not be ambiguous. And I will not accept ambiguity in return.

How to Know Ourselves

Self-awareness is about liberation, not judgment. When we take an honest look at our patterns, wounds, and protection strategies, we reclaim our power. The goal is to be fully seen, and by ourselves first.

Reflect

Start by looking at the patterns that keep showing up, not with shame but with curiosity.

- What's your personal pitfall? What's the behavior or belief that repeats itself in your most important relationships?

- Where do you feel stuck, misunderstood, or like you're not fully seen? Is this a familiar feeling from earlier in life?

- Are you giving away your power to avoid conflict? Or trying to control others as a way to feel safe?

- Can you remember a time you silenced your truth to keep the peace?

Journaling Prompt: *What pattern do you see repeating in your relationships or decisions? What part of you believes this is necessary for love, safety, or belonging?*

Reframe

Awareness is not punishment; it's a return to truth. You don't need to fix yourself to be worthy. You just need to *know* yourself.

- Knowing your patterns doesn't mean you're broken; it means you're awake.

- Self-awareness is not self-blame. It's the doorway to freedom and intentional living.

- You don't need to over-give or self-sacrifice to earn love. Your boundaries are valid. Your needs are sacred.

Mantra: *Knowing my patterns sets me free. I don't have to be perfect to be powerful.*

Reconnect

Knowing yourself is the beginning. Reconnecting to your truth and living with it is the transformation.

- Reflect on recurring relational dynamics. Identify your part with honesty, but also with self-compassion.

- Write a personal contract for how you want to show up moving forward: "I will honor my voice." "I will choose an aligned connection over approval." "I will not betray myself in order to belong."

- Ask for honest feedback from someone you trust: "What's it like to be in a relationship with me?" Use their perspective as a tool, not a verdict.

Affirmation: *I can know my shadow and still be worthy of love, growth, and connection. I am evolving, sacred, and real.*

Final Thought: Self-Knowledge Is Sovereignty

True confidence is honesty.
Not perfection.
Know your gifts.
Lead with purpose.

Know your wounds.
Lead with compassion.
Know your patterns.
Lead with wisdom.

You are not here to fix.
You are here to meet yourself.
Fully and bravely.
Without apology.

Magnetism is truth.
Know who you are.
Live from that knowing.
Stand in your light.

This is Sovereign Living.

KARMA TO DHARMA

"If you want to transform your karma to a more desirable experience, look for the seed of opportunity within every adversity, and tie that seed of opportunity to your dharma, or purpose in life. This will enable you to convert the adversity into a benefit and transform the karma into a totally new expression."

~ Deepak Chopra

The spiritual tradition of India teaches that each of us enters this life to resolve our karma. As described in the Bhagavad Gita, a 700-verse Hindu scripture and sacred text, karma is the universal law of cause and effect. Our actions, thoughts, and intentions ripple forward, creating consequences that shape our future circumstances.

So if you ask, "What is my life's purpose?" the answer is quite straightforward. You need to pay off your karma, so to speak, and follow your dharma, which is the life you are born to live. Dharma is being free from the distraction of pain and suffering so you can achieve ultimate freedom in every aspect of your worldly existence.

You may even show other people the way. You have an opportunity and even a responsibility to share what you've learned. This is the intersection of healing and service. This is how love expands.

My Story: From Setback to Service

One of the most inspiring stories of this from modern history is Helen Keller. Born deaf and blind, she became the first person with those disabilities to graduate college, and she did so with honors. Her life's work was not only personal achievement, it was a collective liberation. She co-founded the ACLU, advocated for the blind, and fought for women's rights.

Helen Keller didn't stop with her own healing. She used her experience to empower others. That is dharma in action.

Along similar lines, Elizabeth Gilbert's book *Eat Pray Love* is another personal journey that turned into a global phenomenon. Gilbert's book offered permission and insight to countless women navigating from heartbreak to rebirth. *Eat Pray Love* was a NY Times Best Selling Book for 187 weeks. The movie grossed $204.6 million worldwide against a $60 million budget. The timing of Gilbert's story aligned to my own journey. Meeting Elizabeth Gilbert at a book signing event and speaking engagement was an epic experience.

This book, **Sovereign Living**, is an expression of my own dharma.

I wrote it because I wished I'd had something like it, a map, a mentor, a guiding voice, when I needed direction most. So this is my offering.

It's a culmination of the lessons I've lived and the truths I've fought for. I've made mistakes. I've taken wrong turns. And I've also returned to my true self again and again. If sharing this helps even one person walk through their own fire, then this work has done its job.

How to Turn Karma (Heal Self) into Dharma (Heal Others)

Your deepest wounds often hold the seeds of your greatest purpose. Karma teaches you. Dharma serves others. When you heal what once hurt you, you gain wisdom and also the power to walk with others through their own dark nights. You don't need to be perfect to be purposeful. You just need to be willing.

Reflect

Transformation begins with reflection. What once broke you might now be your most sacred offering.

- What is the greatest challenge or karmic wound you've moved through in your life?
- What truths did it reveal, not just about your situation, but about your inner strength, patterns, or potential?
- Did anyone support or guide you through it? Was there a person, practice, or resource that lit the way?

Journaling Prompt: *What part of my story once felt heavy, but now holds wisdom? How might it serve someone who's where I once was?*

Reframe

Your karma is not your shame, it's your foundation. Dharma isn't about being a savior. It's about being a mirror, a companion, a light.

- Karmic lessons aren't punishments, they are sacred invitations to evolve, awaken, and embody compassion.
- Dharma doesn't require a platform or profession. It shows up in everyday moments: listening, guiding, sharing, holding space.
- You don't need credentials to be of service. You need authenticity. Your story alone can be medicine.

Mantra: *My wounds have become wisdom. My story is sacred. I serve from love, not perfection.*

Reconnect

Now that you've walked through fire, offer your light. Dharma is simply love in action.

- Give back to the spaces that once held you: volunteer, donate, or support someone walking a similar path.
- Turn your healing into a roadmap. Write down what helped you: the tools, turning points, and truths. Share it with a friend, a blog, or a circle.
- Reach out. Be the one to say, "I've been there too. I don't have all the answers, but I'm here." That offering alone can change a life.

Affirmation: *I transform my healing into service. My past has purpose. I am here to love, guide, and walk with others in truth.*

Final Thought: Let Your Healing Become Someone Else's Hope

Transform your healing into service.
Give your past a purpose.
You are here to love.
You are here to guide.

You did not just survive.
You transformed through it.
That transformation is sacred.
It holds a blueprint.

Someone needs that blueprint.
Share your story.
Share your truth.
Share your light.

Offer it with humility.
Offer it with heart.
Alchemize your past.
Lift others with what you've learned.

This is Sovereign Living.

IMPATIENCE TO PATIENT

*"To lose patience is
to lose the battle."*
~ Mahatma Gandhi

Impatience shows up in our lives as a whisper or a roar. It may be triggered by stress, ambition, anxiety, or even subtle stimuli like caffeine, antidepressants, or overcommitment. But beneath its surface, patience holds an invitation: slow down and listen. Let life reveal its rhythm.

We want answers now, resolution now, healing now. But transformation is rarely instantaneous. It unfolds with grace. It arrives when we are ready, not when we demand.

My Story: Lessons from a Tarot Card and a Cancelled Trip

For years, my sacred Sunday ritual included attending a yoga and meditation class at my teacher Lisa's studio, Forza 5, in Wilton, CT. After each class we drew a tarot card. Week after week, I pulled the same card: Patience.

It became a running joke among our group, but I knew in my bones the card wasn't wrong. I was being handed the lesson I needed most.

I had spent decades rushing toward goals, trying to fix, solve, and achieve. Through yoga, I began to understand that patience is power and trust, not passivity.

That trust was tested just weeks before a dream trip to South India. It was a gift I had planned for my daughter Maddie and me to experience together at the end of her freshman year in college. We were booked, packed, and full of anticipation when the email came: "Trip canceled due to low enrollment."

I was heartbroken. But instead of collapsing, I pivoted. I called Maddie and said, "The bad news is India's off the table. The good news is you get to pick our next destination." Her top choice was Costa Rica.

A yoga teacher named Shiva Rea had been introduced to me during yoga teacher training. While looking on her website for a retreat, I noticed a small logo with a link, a place called Rythmia Life Advancement Center. I'd never heard of it but something drew me in. The Center offered yoga, plant medicine, spa massages, farm-to-table meals and beach proximity. I called, asked a few questions, and booked us right away.

Days later, a man named Haamid called to ask if we could change dates. I declined out of reaction, not reflection, but then reconsidered. I called the next day to say I was willing to be flexible. I was met with the response, "No worries, we've adjusted on our end." A reminder: when you breathe and release, life meets you with grace.

Maddie and I boarded the plane to Costa Rica. En route, I randomly picked up two books by Don Miguel Ruiz: *The Mastery of Self* and *The Mastery of Love*. I had never heard of this author, yet I felt a deep desire to learn what the book titles were offering. I didn't know it then, but choosing those books by Don Miguel Ruiz was a quiet foreshadowing of what would unfold a year later.

When we arrived at the airport in Liberia, Costa Rica, an old SUV with a painted "Rythmia" sign was waiting. As we bounced down dusty roads to Guanacaste, Maddie questioned everything: "You found this place how?" "The reviews said what?"

I smiled and said, "Trust me. I just know it's right." I added, "By the way, there were no reviews."

As the gates opened and beauty greeted us, Maddie turned to me and said, "Okay, I'll shut up now."

Trusting the Timing You Cannot Yet See

Cultivating patience isn't about becoming passive. It's about becoming present. This chapter invites you to turn patience into revelation, allowing your waiting seasons to deepen your faith, not drain your hope.

Reflect

Lack of patience often masks the deeper wisdom. Reflection asks you to slow down and examine what's happening underneath your urgency. Impatience is about what you fear. What is that fear? Naming the root of your agitation allows space for transformation.

- **Identify the Source**
  Where are you clinging, pushing, or rushing for an answer, resolution, or outcome?

- **Name the Root**
  What is truly beneath your impatience? Is it fear, grief, desire, uncertainty, excitement? Naming it brings clarity and softness.

- **Understand the Lesson**
  What is my impatience here to teach me? What is it asking me to notice or to surrender?

Journaling Prompt: *What's really beneath this impatience and what would it feel like to trust instead of push?*

Reframe

Patience is not resignation. It's choosing grace over grasping. It's choosing to believe that things are working out even when they are not visible. Every moment of waiting can become a moment of awakening.

- **Shift the Perspective**
  Patience isn't weakness. It's wisdom cloaked in grace. It takes far more strength to trust than to control.

- **Transform the Energy**
  Turn impatience into trust. Let frustration become a prayer. Gratitude is the bridge that carries you from agitation to peace.

- **Discern What's Yours to Carry**
  Ask Yourself: "Do I have control here?"
  – If yes, take aligned, present action.
  – If not, surrender. The universe is already working behind the scenes.

Mantra: *"Patience Pays. Wait. Let the hand of God work for you. Lean on Him, and all good things will come to you. The One who has made you will take care of you."* ~ Yogi Bhajan

Reconnect

Reconnection is about coming home to the real world, not the fantasy of control or the fear of delay. Your breath is enough. The moment is enough. There is beauty in being where you are, even when you don't yet know where it's leading.

- **Anchor in the Present**
  Sit in stillness. Breathe deeply. Place your hand over your heart. Feel what's true right now and release what's not yours to solve today.

- **Trust the Timing**
  Life is unfolding on time, even if it's not on your moment now. Everything, even now, is working for your good.

- **Create a Grounding Ritual**
  – Light a candle.
  – Take a walk without your phone.
  – Repeat your chosen mantra while placing one hand on your belly, one on your heart.

Affirmation: *I release the need to rush. I trust the unfolding. What is meant for me is already finding its way.*

Final Thought: The Power in the Pause

Patience is quiet trust.
It is faith beyond timelines.
It invites you to pause.
Your dream is not denied.

It is being prepared.
Delays have purpose.
Your soul is catching up.
Destiny is unfolding.

Greet patience as a teacher.
Hand over heart.
Breathe deeply.
Return to center.

You are not behind.
You are becoming.
Alignment is happening.
What's yours is on its way.

This is Sovereign Living.

TURBULENCE TO STILLNESS

*"The quieter you become,
the more you can hear."*

~ *Ram Dass*

This simple yet profound quote captures the essence of true inner stillness. When we quiet the mind, we create sacred space to hear the subtle wisdom within us and also to connect deeply with the world around us.

Stillness doesn't mean the absence of life or chaos. It's the ability to stay calm at the center of it.

But when life feels anything but calm, finding stillness can feel impossible.

My Story: From Storms to Sanctuary

Not long after the devastating loss of my brother, I was thrown into a series of personal storms:

- A turbulent divorce.
- Two of my children stopped speaking to me.
- A job loss.
- A failed rebound relationship.
- A frightening trip to the ICU.

I was dazed, overwhelmed, and deeply disoriented. In the thick of this chaos, I found myself dropping to my knees (on a yoga mat!) whispering to the Universe, *How the hell did I get here?*

Getting onto the yoga mat became my medicine. It was there, breath by breath, that I began learning to re-connect to my body's wisdom, how to slow the mind's relentless chatter, and how to come home to myself. Each practice brought me closer to a fragile but growing sense of life force within me.

That curiosity eventually led me to enroll in a 200-hour Hatha Yoga Teacher Training, not necessarily to teach others, but to heal myself.

In becoming a student again, I stepped out of the "expert" role and into humble, soulful learning.

Now, when turbulence strikes, I meet it with presence. I breathe. I observe. I reset.

I've learned that stillness is a skill. With practice, we all have the power to access it even in the middle of a storm.

Stillness Is Your Superpower

Turbulence is part of life but it doesn't have to define your inner world. Stillness isn't about escaping the storm. It's about learning how to return to your center within it. This chapter invites you to meet overwhelm with presence, shift your state through breath, and find clarity where there was chaos.

Reflect

Reflection is the first step to understanding your stress responses and softening them. Turbulent times can feel like they control us, but often, what's needed is awareness. When you pause to look back with compassion, you begin to see where your true power lies.

- Recall a recent moment of overwhelm or stress.

- What triggered it? An event, a conversation, a thought spiral?
- How did your body respond: shallow breath, quickened pulse, racing thoughts?
- How long did it take to return to calm? Or have you still not completely returned?

Journaling Prompt: *What was my body trying to tell me in that moment of stress and how can I honor it differently next time?*

Reframe

Reframing helps you remember that your breath is not just a bodily function. It's an emotional and spiritual tool. Stillness doesn't require silence around you. It asks for intention within you. You don't have to wait for peace to come from outside. You can create it inside yourself, breath by breath.

- Your breath is a direct line to your nervous system. It offers you a choice: reactivity or rest.
- You don't have to control everything. You only need to regulate *yourself*.
- Stillness is not the absence of difficulty. It's the presence of awareness.

Mantra: *With every breath, I return to balance.*

Practice: Alternate Nostril Breathing (Nadi Shodhana)

This ancient technique balances the left and right hemispheres of the brain and gently calms the nervous system.

1. Sit comfortably. Close your eyes.
2. Use your right thumb to close your right nostril. Inhale slowly through the left.
3. Close the left nostril with your ring finger. Release the thumb. Exhale slowly through the right.
4. Inhale through the right nostril. Close it. Exhale through the left.
5. Continue for 2–5 minutes. Let your breath guide you back to your center.

Mantra: *With every breath, I return to balance.*

Reconnect

Reconnection allows you to revisit a difficult moment, but with stillness rather than stress. The situation may remain but your relationship to it will change. Stillness helps you respond instead of react. It helps you see what's truly yours to carry and what can be released.

- **Revisit the Situation in Your Mind**
  Has your emotional state shifted? Can you see it with more clarity now?

- **Ask Yourself**
  "What wisdom is available to me now that wasn't before?" "What does my calm self know that my stressed self forgot?"

- **An Anchor in the Storm**
  Stillness doesn't eliminate the storm. It anchors you through it. You don't need the world to be quiet to feel peace. You only need to return to yourself. Trust that you can be still, even during chaos.

Affirmation: *In every breath, I find my calm. I return to my center. I trust that I can be still, even here.*

Final Thought: Stillness Is the Superpower

Stillness is not emptiness.
Stillness is a beginning.
It is the sacred pause.
It is the quiet truth.

Stillness lives beyond chaos.
It holds the soft center.
It holds the untouched space.
It holds your inner wisdom.

When life grows loud, pause.
Let your breath be louder.
Let your center be deeper.
Let your stillness be steady.

In stillness, you rise.
In stillness, you soften.
In stillness, you remember.
You remember who you are.

This is Sovereign Living.

HEAVEN TO EARTH

"Heaven on Earth is a choice you must make, not a place you must find."
~ Dr. Wayne Dyer

This quote is a reminder that paradise isn't something we stumble upon or wait for. It's something we choose to create moment by moment. We don't have to chase it, earn it, or escape this life to experience it.

Heaven is not reserved for the afterlife; it's a way of seeing, feeling, and showing up to life right here and right now. When we shift our perception, the sacred reveals itself in even the simplest things.

My Story: From Waiting for Heaven to Living It Now

Growing up Catholic, I was taught that life on Earth was a temporary journey, a sacred passage toward something much greater: Heaven.

Heaven was described to me as a place of eternal peace, where every desire was fulfilled, where souls floated freely from one divine experience to the next.

The path to this paradise was clear:
- Follow the rules.
- Live a good life.
- Uphold the Ten Commandments.
- Be loyal to the Church and family.

And if you faltered? The Church offered the Sacrament of Penance; Confession, forgiveness, and prayers to restore your soul to a state of grace.

I believed in this system. I followed the rituals. And I held fast to the idea that one day, after my death, I would reach this magical perfect place called Heaven.

Until one morning something shifted. Just as I was waking, a radical thought floated into my awareness: *What if heaven isn't where we go after we die? What if heaven is Earth here and now?*

The idea hit me like divine lightning. It wasn't just a comforting thought. It felt like the truth. I could sense my departed loved ones were gathered on a celestial balcony, laughing joyfully, cheering me on: "She figured it out!" That moment changed everything.

I began to live differently. I started witnessing my own life with new eyes. Instead of judging others, I observed myself with compassion. Instead of striving for some distant reward, I began to cherish the reward already around me. I came across a passage from the Gospel of Thomas that deepened this shift: "The realm of the Father is spread out upon the Earth, and people do not see it."

Now I saw it:

In the plants I watered and spoke to with love.

In the spiders I moved gently outside instead of harming.

In the sky, the waves, the sand beneath my feet.

In every hug. Every smile. Every breath.

Heaven is not a faraway paradise we must earn. It is a vibration we can choose. Every day. Every moment.

Choosing Heaven Now

We are taught to believe heaven is somewhere far away, a reward "for later." But heaven is not distant. It's available in every sacred breath, every moment of presence, every act of love. This chapter invites you to stop waiting and start witnessing. What you long for is not "for later." It's for now.

Reflect

Reflection is the doorway to presence. Begin by noticing how you've postponed your joy. You've tied it to a milestone, a future version of yourself, or an external success.

- What joy, truth, or beauty have you been postponing, waiting for "someday"?
- Are you withholding your full presence now, believing fulfillment comes after a goal is reached?
- What might shift if you stopped delaying delight and chose to experience the light right now?

Journaling Prompt: *Where in your life are you waiting for permission to enjoy what is already here?*

Reframe

Reframing allows you to see that heaven is a decision rather than a destination. It's a lens, a way of being. The divine is not out of reach. It lives in every ordinary moment, if you are willing to pause and see it. Nothing needs to change except the way you look at it.

- Heaven isn't a future reward , it's a perspective shift.

- Ask Yourself: "What already feels sacred, beautiful, or divine?"
  – The warmth of a hug.
  – The quiet after rain.
  – A shared laugh.
  – A kind word.
  – A deep breath.

- Let the present moment be enough.
  Heaven doesn't wait.
  It welcomes.

Mantra: *I open my eyes to heaven here and now. Beauty is already around me. Peace is already possible.*

Reconnect

Reconnection is the practice of remembering that the sacred is available in every moment, not just in ritual but in rhythm. Heaven isn't somewhere you arrive. It's something you cultivate. When you slow down and bless what is, you create a life that feels like home to your soul.

- **Create a Ritual of Presence**
  – Say a daily gratitude prayer, simple, heartfelt, true.
  – Walk barefoot in nature. Let the earth remind you that you belong.
  – Light a candle and bless your space with love.
  – Hug like it's holy, with intention and with attention. Let each moment matter (because it does).

- **Be Present in the Now**
  Stop waiting to arrive. You're already here. Let your ordinary life become an extraordinary offering.

Affirmation: *I will experience today, as if I were living in heaven.*

Final Thought: The Realm Within

Choose to awaken.
Heaven is here.
It lives in your heart.
It lives in your breath.

You are not seeking heaven.
You are remembering it.
You are returning inward.
You are coming home.

Pause today.
Smile at the sky.
Savor your food.
Feel the hug longer.

Watch the light spill in.
Whisper the truth.
"This is heaven."
"I am home."

This is Sovereign Living.

POSSESSIONS TO GIFTS

*"There is nothing about
a caterpillar that tells you
it's going to be a butterfly."*
~ R. Buckminster Fuller

This quote reminds us that transformation often hides beneath the surface. We can't always see the growth that's happening, or the purpose behind loss, until we look back and realize that what we thought was the end was really a beginning.

Possessions, like people, are often mistaken for permanent fixtures in our lives. But they're gifts. Temporary, beautiful, sometimes heartbreaking, always evolving. When we release the illusion of control or ownership, we make space for what's next.

My Story: Releasing the Car, Receiving the Gifts

My love for cars was inspired by my father, who seemed to have a new sports car every few years. In my memory, his favorite was always the Ford Mustang, both the classic three-speed and later the five-speed. Driving out to the airport with him on a Sunday, parking beneath the flight path to watch planes soar overhead, remains one of my favorite driving experiences and most cherished memories with him.

When, I made a cross-country move that required me to let go of many possessions, including my beloved Audi A5 convertible my heart skipped a beat. It wasn't just a car. It was a symbol of success, freedom, and refined engineering. I loved the feel of the wheel, the sun on my face, the way it hugged curves on rural and coastal roads. Saying goodbye felt like losing a piece of myself.

But the moment I let go, something surprising happened.

First, my employer handed me the keys to an all black Porsche 911 convertible. It was sleek, luxurious, and unexpected. Then, I gifted the Audi to my daughter, who was heading off to college. Watching her drive it away was a moment of pure love and release. Later, when I was ready to purchase again, a car allowance arrived and enabled me to upgrade to a brand-new BMW convertible.

What I learned is this: when you release with trust, the universe returns with grace.

Even more profound than cars are the people we try to hold onto. I've experienced the grief of letting go, especially in relationships I believed would last forever. But people, like possessions, are not ours to keep. They are ours to experience. To learn from. To love and release with reverence when the time comes.

Letting Go to Let Life In

Holding on too tightly can close the very doors you're meant to walk through. Sometimes what you think you're protecting is actually what's preventing your peace. This chapter invites you to soften your grip on outcomes, identities, and attachments. Trust that when you let go, you don't lose control. You gain alignment.

Reflect

Reflection helps you identify the places in your life

where grasping has replaced grace. Are you clinging from fear, from habit, or from some meaning assigned long ago? Often it's not the thing itself that keeps us stuck. It's what we've decided it means. Awareness creates room for surrender.

- What are you holding too tightly? Is it an identity, a relationship, a possession, a belief?
- Ask Yourself: "What am I afraid will happen if I let go?"
- Are you attached to the thing itself or to what it symbolizes?

Journaling Prompt: *What's something I once lost that made space for something better? What did I learn from that shift?*

Reframe

Reframing lets you shift from ownership to appreciation. Everything in your life is a gift, not a guarantee. Releasing doesn't mean erasing. It means honoring what was and making space for what's next. You can love fully without holding tightly.

- Shift from "This is mine" to "This was a gift I got to experience."
- Let gratitude replace grasping.
- Honor what someone or something brought into your life even if their chapter is complete.

Mantra: *I release what no longer serves me and trust something greater is on its way.*

Reconnect

Reconnection is about replacing attachment with presence. When you love with openness, not ownership, you create space for true connection, with others, with life, and with yourself. Freedom is not the absence of care. It is the absence of control.

- **Ask Yourself**
  "Am I loving this person or clinging to who I want them to be?" "Am I gripping this path or walking it with trust?"

- **Honor Diverging Paths**
  Let go with blessing. Trust that honoring another's journey does not diminish your own.

- **Practice a Ritual of Release**
  Write a short letter of gratitude and release to someone or something you're ready to hold more lightly. Let it be your offering of freedom, for them and for you.

Affirmation: *I open my hands. I open my heart. I trust that letting go makes space for what is true.*

Final Thought: Open Hands, Open Heart

Possessions fade over time.
People grow and change.
Seasons shift with grace.
Life keeps moving forward.

Love without holding tight.
Release without any fear.
Trust what life reveals.
This is your true power.

Hold nothing too tightly.
Celebrate every sacred gift.
Honor what gently arrives.
Bless what softly leaves.

What's yours will stay.
What's yours will grow.
What's yours will return.
Live with open hands, always.

This is Sovereign Living.

RESIST TO SURRENDER

"Surrender happens spontaneously with the knowledge that you are not in control of anything, not even your thoughts or feelings. When you realize that you are not in control of your life, but some supreme law governs life, then surrender happens."
~ *Gurudev Sri Sri Ravi Shankar*

True surrender is the boldest act of self-liberation. It is choosing to lay down an illusion of control and open your heart to divine orchestration.

Yet in its own way surrender is an act of control in the best sense of the word. This kind of surrender is the opposite of defeat.

Surrender does not mean you stop showing up. You still take action, speak your truth, and tend your garden. But when you surrender the outcome, you invite grace to do its part. You allow life to co-create with you.

If resistance is your old armor, surrender is your sacred trust.

My Story: From Gripping to Trusting

For most of my adult life, I held tightly to plans, outcomes, and people. I believed that if I tried hard, stayed alert, stayed busy, stayed prepared, I could outmaneuver disappointment.

But life had its own plan:
- The untimely deaths of my younger siblings.

- The loss of my father.
- The loss of relationships, personal and professional.

Each time, I thought I was falling apart. And in some ways, I was. But in deeper ways, I was falling into the arms of surrender.

When I finally stopped resisting the pain and began listening for its wisdom, I softened. I began to see that the love I was chasing had always lived inside me. That freedom, my deepest desire, wasn't something to earn. It was something to remember.

I stopped pushing.
I stopped controlling.
And I started allowing.

Now I don't chase people or plans. I magnetize them. I live with open hands. And in doing so, everything meant for me flows toward me with peace, not panic.

The Strength of Surrendering to the Unseen

Resistance is often a response to fear of losing control, of being disappointed, of being asked to wait. But what if the unknown isn't a threat, it's a threshold? This chapter invites you to soften your grip on outcomes, trust what you cannot yet see, and allow grace to carry what your mind can't hold. Surrender is not a failure of effort, it's the highest form of wisdom.

Reflect

Reflection allows you to notice where tension is still alive in your thoughts, your body, your heart. Resistance often shows up as control, urgency, or a clenched desire to make something happen.

Try naming what you're trying to force, and why:

- Where in your life are you still resisting a truth, a change, a call to trust?

- What outcome, desire, or situation are you gripping tightly?

- Ask Yourself: "Why am I trying to control what I have no control over?"

Journaling Prompt: *What am I resisting right now, and what is that costing me, emotionally, spiritually, or energetically?*

Reframe

Reframing invites you to replace the myth of control with the medicine of trust. Surrender is not failure. You are stepping into partnership with something wiser and more loving than your fear. Resistance contracts. Surrender expands. The outcome may still be unknown, but your posture can shift from tightness to trust.

- Let go of this belief: "If I don't control it, I'll lose it." Replace it with: "If I trust, what's meant for me will stay and what's not will gently fall away."

- Surrender isn't weakness. It's strength in partnership with divine timing and guidance.

- You're not giving up. You're giving over to love, to grace, and to your soul's deeper rhythm.

Mantra: *I release control. I allow love, guidance, and grace to lead.*

Reconnect

Reconnection is about returning to the wisdom that already lives within you. That wisdom is not the voice of fear, but the whisper of intuition. When you release the need to know everything, you make space for true knowing to emerge. The answers may not come instantly, but the peace will.

- **When Fear or Urgency Rises, Return to Presence**
  Let your body become the altar. Let stillness become the prayer. Here's a simple five-step practice:
  1. Sit quietly with eyes closed.
  2. Rest both palms open on your lap as a gesture of trust.
  3. Breathe deeply and slowly.
  4. Whisper: "Why have you placed this desire inside my heart?" "What would you have me do next?"
  5. Listen. Wait. The response may come in a word, a symbol, a breath, or a quiet sense of peace.

Affirmation: *I trust what I cannot yet see. I surrender to what is true, aligned, and guided by love.*

Final Thought: Where Resistance Ends and Freedom Begins

Surrender begins your freedom.
It does not end your strength.
Release the tight grip.
Let life move toward you.

What you release reveals you.
Let your heart soften.
Let your breath slow.
Let fear loosen its hold.

You need not push destiny.
Let destiny rise to meet you.
Trust the timing unseen.
Trust the unfolding unknown.

Nothing meant for you requires force.
Surrender takes quiet courage.
Choose alignment over anxiety.
Choose peace over pressure.

This is Sovereign Living.

Part Two

QUEENSHIP
AWAKEN YOUR ROYAL SELF THROUGH EMPOWERED & AUTHENTIC LIVING

Queenship is the art of stepping fully into your Sovereignty, no longer defined by others, but established from within. It is the sacred passage from woman to women from isolation to sisterhood, from independence to interdependence. Here, you rise not alone, but together.

In **Woman to Women**, you awaken to the power of collective elevation learning that true queens lift one another, celebrating rather than comparing.

Servant to Queen invites you to trade people-pleasing for purpose, and obligation for ownership to lead not from hierarchy, but from heart. Through **Jealousy to Admiration**, envy becomes inspiration, and comparison transforms into connection. You realize that another woman's light does not dim yours; it amplifies it.

In **Damsel in Distress to Wonder Woman**, you reclaim your agency. You stop waiting to be rescued and remember that you have always been the hero of your own story. **Giving to Receiving** teaches that receptivity is not weakness, it is balance. You learn to open your palms as well as your heart, allowing abundance to flow both ways.

In **Indecisive to Internal Knowing**, you return to the still, wise voice within the inner compass that never leads astray when trust replaces doubt. **Perception to Reality** is the shift from illusion to embodiment, where you stop seeing life through fear's distortion and begin perceiving it through truth's clarity.

Through **Identity Crisis to Identity Creation**, you realize you are not who the world told you to be, you are who you consciously choose to become. **Judgment to Judgment Detox** is your liberation from the inner critic. You cleanse the mind of comparison and criticism, creating space for compassion, toward self and others alike.

In **Seeking Happiness to Being Happiness**, joy is no longer a destination but a state of being. You stop searching for fulfillment and begin radiating it. **Blind to Seeing** opens the eyes of your soul. You move from distraction to discernment, from glancing to gazing, seeing not with the mind, but with presence and reverence.

Finally, **Wearing Clothes to Curating a Signature Look** transforms style into Sovereignty, every fabric, color, and detail becoming a reflection of your essence, a visual expression of authenticity and grace.

Queenship is the embodiment of wisdom in motion, where confidence meets compassion, and elegance merges with empowerment. It is the reclamation of your divine authority, the remembering that you were never meant to fit in, you were born to reign.

WOMAN TO WOMEN

"Be the woman who fixes another woman's Crown without telling the world it was crooked."

~ Amy Morin

We are entering an era where collaboration is far more powerful than competition. But to truly evolve, we must acknowledge the cultural inheritance we carry as women and choose a new path.

Many of us were raised by mothers who marched for rights we now take for granted. They told us to get educated, earn our own money, and never depend on anyone else. And while that strength built new foundations, it often came with side effects. Scarcity thinking. Thinking that if one woman wins, another must lose.

But the opposite is true. When one woman rises, we all rise.

My Story: From Rivalry to Rise

I saw this dynamic play out clearly in the workplace.

A female colleague of mine, whom I would describe as intelligent, stylish, and self-assured, with an energy that commands attention without ever asking for it, was caught in a power struggle that had nothing to do with her work. It had everything to do with someone else's ego. After ending a relationship with a male colleague, she was suddenly being undermined by, her boss who began dating that same man.

My colleague, once joyful and confident, began to shrink. Eventually, she left the company altogether. Not surprisingly, her former boss's relationship ended, her position dissolved, and no one won.

Observing this, I realized then what I already knew deep down: tearing another woman down never creates more power; it drains it. Every time we engage in comparison or silent resentment, we reinforce the false belief that only one of us can succeed.

But when we support each other boldly and without condition, we create abundance in our personal work and workplace, our friendships, and our communities.

Women Rising Together

Comparison is a thief of joy and connection. When we compare, we isolate. When we celebrate, we build something sacred. This chapter invites you to shift from quiet competition to collaboration. When one woman rises, it's not a threat, it's a mirror. The same light lives in you.

Reflect

Reflection invites you to take an honest look at how subtle comparison may be impacting your relationships with other women. The voice of competition is often quiet, but cloaked in insecurity and judgment:

- Are you subtly competing with, rather than celebrating, other women?
- When another woman shines, do you feel inspired, or slightly diminished?

- Where might quiet comparison, self-doubt, or withheld celebration be blocking your capacity for real sisterhood?

Journaling Prompt: *Where in my life am I withholding celebration or support for another woman and what's the story behind it?*

Reframe

Reframing allows you to see that sisterhood is not a scarcity game. It's a sacred circle. Another woman's power doesn't diminish yours. It affirms what's possible. True empowerment multiplies when it's shared freely, without performance or pretense.

- Sisterhood is not a threat, it's sacred.
- Imagine what becomes possible when we choose connection over quiet rivalry.
- There is enough space, enough success, and enough light for all of us to rise.

Mantra: *When one woman rises, we all rise.*

Reconnect

Reconnection is the daily practice of choosing collaboration over comparison. But the village you long for may not arrive on its own. It must be built with intention, vulnerability, and love. Start small. Start now.

- **Build the Village Intentionally**
  Choose three women this week to support with presence and sincerity:

- Send a thoughtful message of affirmation or encouragement
- Share a resource, opportunity, or uplifting story
- Invite them into a moment of joy, reflection, or ritual

- **Take the Action**
  Don't wait for a crisis to show up for one another. Let support become your lifestyle. Not just a gesture, but a rhythm.

Affirmation: *I choose connection over comparison. I rise with others, not in spite of them. Sisterhood is my strength.*

Final Thought: The Power of Unshakable Sisterhood

A rising tide lifts everyone.
We rise together, always.
Light the candle.
Share the flame.

Rewrite the narrative.
Choose celebration over scarcity.
Choose unity over competition.
Choose support over silence.

Stand shoulder to shoulder.
In boardrooms and living rooms.
In birthing rooms too.
Stand with full hearts.

Teach our daughters trust.
Teach them sisterhood.
Sovereignty is shared.
Sovereignty is collective.

This is Sovereign Living.

*"Fix her Crown quietly.
Celebrate her loudly.
Build an empire together."*
~ Laura Alfano

SERVANT TO QUEEN

"The strength of a realm comes from its King; the strength of the King comes from his Queen."
~ Cody Edward Lee Miller

Throughout history, women have been revered as nurturers, caretakers, and anchors of family life. But too often that reverence has translated into an image of quiet servitude. Many women unknowingly slipped into the role of servant, putting the needs of everyone else first, and leaving themselves last.

Yet true feminine power doesn't lie in sacrificing yourself endlessly. It lies in remembering your Sovereignty. While being a Queen doesn't mean ruling others, it does mean honoring your own worth and allowing others to do the same. It's the difference between doing it all to being fully you.

My Story: Choosing Yourself Isn't Selfish, It's Sovereign

After my divorce, I began dating again. None of the relationships turned out to be the "one", but I realized that post-divorce dating, especially as a mother, carried a unique kind of freedom. The pressure to "build a family" was gone. I no longer felt obligated to stay in a relationship that wasn't working. That was liberating.

With an open heart I entered relationships and saw them as opportunities for self-discovery. These experiences taught me how I communicate, what my boundaries are, how I receive and express love, and whether I was growing through this connection.

I asked myself: *What feels aligned and what doesn't? Am I speaking up for what I need?*

Men always mirrored something back to me, sometimes healing and sometimes challenging.

One unexpected gift of dating was meeting families. Watching how a man interacts with his parents, siblings, former partners, or children reveals so much. I often found myself gravitating toward the women, mothers, sisters, even ex-wives, who tended to share more openly and emotionally.

But it was one man's mother who truly shifted something in me.

She was a radiant woman in her 80s, always in bright colors, bold lipstick, with perfectly coiffed hair and long, polished nails. Her energy was magnetic. My boyfriend always included me in his visits with her, and I loved watching their dynamic.

One Sunday morning at brunch with his family, he casually shared a bit about my life. "Laura has three kids," he said. "While she was raising them, she also worked full-time and made them three meals a day."

His mother turned toward me and said warmly, "Darling, I imagine you were a wonderful mother and wife."

Then her son responded, with a slightly pointed tone, "Mom, you stayed home, but left us with sitters to go to movie premieres with dad. You never cooked, not once. We ate pizza, cereal, whatever we could find. Five kids and we just figured it out."

Without missing a beat, she replied, unapologetically:

"Dear son, your father was everything to me. He wanted me by his side at those events. We had a beautiful marriage and gave you a wonderful life. You all turned out more than fine. And yes, you learned to cook for yourselves. What a useful skill. What exactly are you complaining about?"

Then she turned to me and delivered the line that shifted something deep within me:

"Darling, my husband was a king, and I was his queen. If I had spent all my time cooking, cleaning, and tending to the children, I would have been a servant, not a queen. A queen is loved, honored, and prioritized. And because I lived that way, my children and grandchildren now treat me like a queen too."

She wasn't advocating neglect. She was modeling balance. She reminded me that when we step fully into our worth, we invite others to do the same. Her story wasn't about rejecting motherhood, but about choosing partnership and presence with intention.

That was an "aha" moment for me. Too often, women carry the mental, emotional, and physical load of family life, not because they must, but because they feel they should. We serve, support, nurture, and sometimes forget to expect love and reverence in return.

Culturally, women have been conditioned that way.

According to the Bureau of Labor Statistics, in 1967, about 49% of U.S. mothers were stay-at-home moms. That number dropped steadily, reaching a low of 23% in 1999 as women pursued careers and independence.

But recently there has been a gentle uptick: By 2024, the number has risen to 26%, driven largely by high childcare costs and a renewed appreciation for home life. Covid-19 may have also contributed to the marginal increase.

But we've never had a clear roadmap for how to simultaneously balance a career, marriage, and children. Something always had to give. And while some women chose to pour themselves into motherhood, others prioritized their marriages. Men, too, began stepping into new roles, showing up more fully as co-parents and partners, evolving from the distant "provider" model many of their own fathers embodied.

Today we're witnessing a shift toward shared responsibility. More couples work from home. Parenting is becoming more collaborative. Couples are reclaiming time for one another, not just for the kids.

As I reflect on this journey, I tell the young mothers around me there is no one right way. Do what aligns with your values. Choose to work full-time, part-time, or stay home. But don't forget to prioritize your marriage.

Children thrive when they feel the security of their parents' love directed at them, but also toward each other. They don't need perfection. They need presence. And often, that presence begins with you remembering your own worth.

You are not just a mother. Not just a partner. You are a Queen. A queen leads with love, not sacrifice.

Claiming the Crown Over Self-Sacrifice

There is a version of service that uplifts and there is a version that depletes. Many women are conditioned to give endlessly, to wear sacrifice as a badge of honor. But true Sovereignty is found in balance, not burnout.

This chapter invites you to rise from duty into dignity, to stop abandoning yourself in the name of care, and to wear your Crown with clarity, grace, and unapologetic worth.

Reflect

Reflection helps you explore the roles you've taken on, consciously or unconsciously, in your relationships. Caregiving, nurturing, and leading are powerful expressions of love. But when they come at the cost of your own well-being, they become cages instead of Crowns.

- How do you see yourself in your closest relationships? Caregiver, fixer, nurturer, leader, Queen?
- Where in your life do you feel like you're constantly serving without being replenished in return?
- What beliefs, upbringing, or cultural messages taught you that others' needs come before you own?

Journaling Prompt: *Where in my life am I still operating from duty, rather than from worth?*

Reframe

Honoring yourself is not selfish, it's Sovereign. The Queen archetype is about reigning with self-respect, sacred boundaries, and emotional maturity. You are allowed to receive. You are allowed to rest. You are allowed to rise.

- Serving with love is noble, but not at the cost of self-abandonment.
- Being a Queen means honoring your own needs with the same devotion you offer others.
- You can nurture and receive. You can support and be supported. This is not a contradiction; it is wholeness.

Empowering Question: *What small but powerful shifts can I make today to step more fully into my queenship?*

– Ask for help.
– Set a boundary.
– Receive without guilt.
– Speak your needs clearly.
– Choose joy over obligation.

Reconnect

Reconnection is about occupying your full worth and inviting others to meet you there. When you lead from wholeness you don't need to be everything for everyone. You show others what it means to live with grace, strength, and self-respect.

- **Invite Your Circle In**
  Let others witness the woman you are becoming. Don't dim your light for comfort. Share your truth, with love and clarity.

- **Model Sovereign Self-Leadership**
  Communicate your needs. Celebrate your milestones. Receive compliments, care, and praise without apology.

- **Celebrate Yourself**
  Not as a reward, but as a rhythm. Let your life reflect your worth before anyone else does.

Affirmation: *I am a Queen. I honor my worth, I receive with grace, and I inspire others to rise with me.*

Final Thought: Your Throne Is Waiting

A Queen does not control.
A Queen does not perform perfection.
A Queen comes home to herself.
She rests in her own truth.

She releases old guilt.
She lets her body soften.
She welcomes support with grace.
She receives what nurtures her.

She lives her boundaries beautifully.
She radiates joy naturally.
And others rise beside her.
Her presence becomes permission.

Your family needs your radiance.
Your world needs your peace.
Your community needs your joy.
Your throne has always been waiting.

This is Sovereign Living.

JEALOUSY TO ADMIRATION

> *"Never hate jealous people.*
> *They are jealous because*
> *they think you're*
> *better than them."*
> ~ *Paulo Coelho*

Jealousy is one of the most human emotions and one of the most misunderstood. It often shows up when we're not feeling rooted in our own self-worth or when someone else's life reflects a version of success we haven't yet claimed.

Jealousy can be uncomfortable but it isn't inherently bad. It can be a powerful teacher. When met with awareness, jealousy can act as a mirror, revealing our deepest desires and unhealed wounds.

What we admire in others is often what we are longing to unlock within ourselves. We grow when we move from envy to elevation. Jealousy can become fuel, not fire.

My Story: Learning to Rise by Celebrating the Women Who Already Have

There was a time in my life during my divorce and the years that followed when I felt triggered by women who appeared to have it all together. Women who had an adoring husband, children fully present, a successful career, and unshakable confidence. I'd see them thriving while I felt like I was piecing myself together in slow motion.

But instead of spiraling into shame, I got curious.
- What were they doing differently?
- How were they prioritizing their joy?
- What daily rituals or boundaries had they established that I had been neglecting?

I began asking them questions, not with resentment but with respect. Most of them were more than willing to share. I learned that many had weathered their own storms. They weren't perfect; they were persistent.

I released my low grade jealousy and chose admiration instead. Then something powerful happened, my own confidence rose. My sense of worth deepened. I realized I didn't want their lives, I wanted my own life to be fully realized. That clarity changed everything.

Shifting from Comparison to Expansion

Jealousy is not a flaw, it's a flag. It's a signal that something within you is being stirred, awakened, or waiting to be expressed. When you meet that feeling with curiosity instead of shame, you gain access to your own untapped potential. This chapter invites you to alchemize envy into admiration and turn comparison into motivation.

Reflect

Reflection allows you to look beneath the surface of jealousy. The emotion itself is not wrong. It often reveals a deep longing, a waking dream, or a quality you're ready to claim for yourself. Begin with real honesty:

- Who have you felt jealous of recently?

- What specifically triggered that feeling? Was it their relationship, success, confidence, ease, or lifestyle?

- What quality in them are you truly admiring and what does it awaken in you?

Journaling Prompt: *What desire or potential in me is being stirred by this feeling? What is it asking me to notice or nurture?*

Reframe

Reframing allows you to shift jealousy from self-judgment into soul guidance. What you admire in someone else is not proof that you've failed. It's proof that something similar may be possible for you. Let their light become your map, not your shadow.

- Jealousy is not always a sign of lack. It can be a signal of longing, a desire waiting for permission.

- Instead of seeing their success as a threat, see it as proof that it can be done.

- Ask yourself: "What habits, choices, or mindset might I learn from their journey?"

Insight Practice: *Recall a time you turned comparison into motivation. What did you do differently and what was the outcome? How did your energy shift when you focused on your own path with clarity and courage?*

Reconnect

Reconnection is the moment when you consciously choose to celebrate others as a way to expand yourself. The energy you pour into admiration rather than comparison uplifts everyone, including yourself. Sisterhood, expansion, and Sovereignty are built there.

- **Choose Admiration Consciously**
  Let others' greatness be a mirror, not a measuring stick. Use their light to reveal your own.

- **Celebrate Over Compete**
  Text someone your appreciation. Compliment a peer's work. Speak admiration out loud. Watch how your own energy expands.

- **Anchor the Shift**
  The more you celebrate what you see in others, the more you awaken what's waiting in you.

Affirmation: *I admire the greatness in others as a reflection of what is rising within me. There is no lack only limitless possibility.*

Final Thought: From Comparison to Inspiration

Admire her and rise higher.
Celebrate her and shine brighter.
Her glow expands your own light.
Your radiance grows with hers.

Comparison drains your power quickly.
Inspiration amplifies your strength.
Jealousy is a needless detour.
Admiration is a sacred portal.

What you see in her lives within.
Recognition reveals your reflection.
Her greatness mirrors your potential.
Let it call you higher still.

Choose admiration over quiet envy.
Choose expansion over shrinking fear.
If she can have it,
So can you, beautifully.

This is Sovereign Living.

DAMSEL IN DISTRESS TO WONDER WOMAN

"She was powerful not because she wasn't scared, but because she went on so strongly, despite the fear."

~ Atticus

At some point in life we each face the choice: Do I crumble under the weight of chaos, or do I rise to meet it with clarity and grace?

Women have long been conditioned to lean helplessly on others or to silently carry the world on their shoulders. Neither archetype of damsel in distress or martyr captures the truth of who we are.

Sovereign women meet life's demands with discernment, strategy, intuition, and unwavering self-trust. We don't fake strength. We cultivate it to honor the inner knowing that we are capable beyond measure.

My Story: The Shift from Mission Control to Inner Command

In my early 40's I was married with three super active children and a full-time career. My cup and my heart were truly full. I lived in a neighborhood where most of the mothers stayed home, but I was determined to be the mother who could do it all and do it well.

My children were always dressed, fed, well-organized, and prepared. I ran the house like a mission control center. There was a color-coded calendar on the counter, perfectly timed drop-offs and pick-ups, school forms signed, and cheerleading chants offered at the door. I loved it. It gave me purpose, pride, and momentum.

But behind the scenes, I was constantly measuring and managing. And I sometimes judged those who didn't have the same rhythm. When I saw mothers frantic at school pickup, or kids unprepared and stressed, a thought would pass through my mind: *What do you do all day?*

Still, I knew this was my superpower: I could anticipate, organize, and execute with precision. That same clarity carried over to my work in the corporate world. I thrived on being the go-to woman during times of crisis.

I remember being called into the office of the North American President of the global skincare company I was working for. Bill sat me down and in a serious tone, he said, "We do not have a new product launch planned during peak season for our portfolio of brands." He handed me a competitor's corporate group event ad, saying, "We need a big bang to start the year, or we're not going to hit our Q1 target."

Without hesitation I responded, "I've got this." And I did. I assembled a dream team, mapped out the launch plan, partnered with Big Brothers Big Sisters and we delivered. We exceeded every target and proved what was possible when power is deployed with poise and purpose.

That was a turning point. I wasn't proving anything anymore. I was simply being who I was born to be: not a damsel hoping to be rescued, but a Sovereign woman building an enterprise.

Step Into Your Power and Practice Self-Leadership

Self-leadership begins when you stop waiting and start trusting. It's not about controlling every outcome, it's about showing up in full ownership of your choices, your voice, and your truth. In every moment you reclaim your power from doubt, distraction, or dependency, you step deeper into your Sovereignty. This chapter invites you to move from reaction to responsibility, from seeking validation to standing in quiet, embodied wisdom.

Reflect

Reflection allows you to witness the habits and stories that shape how you respond to challenge and choice. Often, we give our power away by waiting, deferring, or shrinking.

Self-leadership begins when you stop waiting and start trusting. It means showing up in full ownership of your choices, your voice, and your truth. It's reclaiming your power from doubt, distraction, or dependency.

- In times of stress or uncertainty, do you lead or retreat?
- What does your response say about how much you trust yourself?
- Are you waiting for someone else to save you; a partner, boss, mentor or friend?

Journaling Prompt: *Where in my life am I outsourcing power that is mine to claim?*

Reframe

Reframing helps you move from fear to freedom. You don't need to discover your power, you only need to remember it. You know how to listen and respond with integrity. Moments of uncertainty are invitations to lead, not from ego but from essence.

- Reclaim your power not with pressure, but with grounded self-worth.
- Ask yourself: "Am I seeking advice to gain clarity or because I fear making the wrong choice?"
- True strength isn't loud. It's the quiet confidence of trusting your own wisdom.

Empowering Question: *What would shift if I moved from seeking approval to trusting my inner voice?*

Reconnect

Reconnection means returning to the wisdom within you and acting from it daily. Self-leadership is about presence. You embody your power and you lead by example.

- **Find Inspiration**
  - Think of a woman you admire for her strength.
  - What qualities does she embody?
  - Where and how can you begin to practice those qualities?

- **Name Your Superpower**
  - What's the unique way you naturally lead, love, create, or guide?
  - Is it your clarity? Your warmth? Your vision? Your steadiness?

– Let that superpower guide how you speak, decide, and show up every day.

Affirmation: *I trust my intuition. I lead with strength and softness. I am not waiting to be saved. I already have everything I need to rise.*

Final Thought: The Power of Self-Trust

You don't need a cape.
You already wear a Crown.
Stop waiting for rescue.
You are your own hero.

Trust your intuition deeply.
Lead with strength and softness.
You are not waiting.
You are rising now.

Strength is not loud.
Strength is not frantic.
It speaks through calm clarity.
It moves with quiet confidence.

The world needs no damsels.
It needs Crowned Wonder Women.
Women who lift others.
Women who never lose themselves.

This is Sovereign Living.

GIVING TO RECEIVING

"Most women are starving to receive something that they need to give to themselves."
~ Sherry Argov

Women are praised for being selfless, nurturing, and endlessly available. Giving is seen as virtuous. But receiving? That can be viewed as selfish, indulgent, or weak.

But receiving is actually the essence of feminine energy. As women, we are biologically, energetically, and spiritually wired to receive with grace and beauty. But many of us have been conditioned to suppress this gift. We give until we're depleted. We offer help, love, time, money, and advice. And when someone wants to give back? We resist. Shrink. Deflect.

We block what we deeply crave: to be supported, held, nourished.

My Story: Receiving Isn't Weakness, It's Sacred, and Strong

In my earlier relationships, I gave freely; love, forgiveness, time, attention. But receiving never came as easily. Even when a man opened a door for me, I'd feel a subtle twinge of discomfort, as if allowing it made me less independent.

Then one day, it clicked.

I was listening to a podcast that referenced our actual physical design. As a heterosexual woman I suddenly saw the metaphor in our anatomy. Men are wired to give. Women are designed to receive, physically, emotionally, spiritually, and energetically. We are meant to receive deeply, and then to alchemize what we've received into something even greater. This is not weakness, it's our power.

As someone once said: "Give a woman a seed, and she'll give you a garden. Give her a house, and she'll make it a home. Give her groceries, and she'll prepare a meal. Give her sperm, and she'll create a child. Give her love, and she'll return it with even more."

Women can multiply and elevate what we are given. We take the raw materials of life and create something more meaningful, beautiful, or complete from them.

Awareness of this shifted something profound in me. I began experimenting with small moments: allowing a man to carry my groceries, letting a compliment land without deflection, accepting help without explanation or apology.

And the more I received with grace, the more men leaned in. They felt needed, respected, honored. And I felt held, not because I couldn't do things on my own, but because I didn't have to.

Receiving became my new form of self-respect. And in turn, it became my greatest magnetism.

The Power of Receiving

Giving may come naturally. Receiving can feel unfamiliar, even uncomfortable. Yet true connection requires both. Receiving isn't a weakness. It ought to be an act of trust. It says, "I am open. I am worthy. I am willing to be nourished." This chapter invites you to soften the walls around your heart to let love, care, and support move freely from you and to you.

Reflect

Reflection helps you examine the deeply rooted beliefs you may attach to receiving. For many this stirs guilt, discomfort, and a sense of indebtedness.

- What is your current relationship with receiving?
- Do you feel guilt, awkwardness, or comfort when someone offers love, help, or kindness?
- Think of a recent moment when someone gave you a compliment, a gift, or words of support.
  – How did you respond?
  – What emotions came up?

Journaling Prompt: *What do my reactions to receiving reveal about my beliefs around worthiness or independence?*

Reframe

Reframing allows you to see receiving not as passivity, but as sacred participation. In many spiritual traditions, especially feminine ones , receptivity is not optional. It is essential. You were never meant to pour out endlessly without being filled.

- Receiving is not a weakness. It's a vital part of connection and feminine energy.
- Let go of the belief that you must earn support or prove your value to be cared for.
- How do you want to feel when you receive?
  – Safe?

- Seen?
- Soft?
- Grateful?

Those feelings are not rewards. They are your feminine birthrights.

Empowering Thought: *Receiving is not taking it's allowing love to flow both ways.*

Reconnect

Reconnection is allowing love to flow both ways. Receiving with grace affirms your worth and mirrors that worth to others. You teach the world how to love you well.

- **Practice Receptive Energy Intentionally**
  Ask: "What is one small thing I can receive today without guilt or apology?"
  - A kind word
  - A helping hand
  - A compliment
  - Rest
  - Pleasure
  - Praise

- **Let "Thank You" Be Enough**
  Resist the urge to deflect, minimize, or repay. Simply receive. Let the gift land.

- **Tune Into the Shift**
  Notice how your body and spirit respond when you allow yourself to be nourished.

Affirmation: *I receive with open arms, an open heart, and deep gratitude. I am worthy of love, care, and support just as I am.*

Final Thought: Receiving Is an Act of Power, Not Passivity

To receive is to trust life.
To receive is to open.
To receive is to allow.
To receive is to believe.

I am open and worthy.
I am ready to receive.
Let yourself be filled fully.
Teach the world loving giving.

Receiving is not losing power.
Receiving is standing in it.
Rest in your feminine nature.
Honor your body's ancient wisdom.

Let go of proving.
Let go of repaying.
Receive with an open heart.
Let abundance complete its circle.

This is Sovereign Living.

INDECISIVE TO INTERNAL KNOWING

"Be established within yourself."
~ Yogi Bhajan

Why is it so easy to ask everyone else what we should do? Why is it so hard to ask and trust ourselves?

It's natural to seek advice now and then. But indecision occurs when we look outward for validation instead of inward for clarity.

No one else lives your life, feels your emotions, or walks your path. Only you can decide what is truly aligned with your heart and values.

My Story: Why the Strongest Decisions Come From Within, Not Around You

A close friend of mine spent years in a loving but complicated relationship. She and her boyfriend had deep chemistry, shared passions for surfing and fitness, and adored each other's families. But their careers kept them in different cities.

Every few months emotional waves would crash in and (again) they'd break up. My friend would call me, feeling overwhelmed: "What should I do?" We'd talk, but she'd also consult everyone else she knew, even casual friends. Eventually I asked her, "What do you think you should do?"

When she repeated what others had told her, I asked again. This time, she paused, took a breath, and said, "I think I need to take some time alone to think."

That moment was her turning point. She spent a few

days reflecting, journaling, and grounding herself. She realized her indecision had little to do with the relationship and everything to do with work pressure, sleepless nights, and neglecting her own needs. She reached out to repair things but her partner wasn't ready.

Four months passed before she heard from him. By then she was no longer desperate for an answer. She had evolved. She herself was the answer. In time, they reconciled with clear goals and healthier communication. Two years later they made a choice to live in the same city to begin building a life together.

Coming Home to Your Own Voice

In a world of noise, advice, and endless opinions, it's easy to lose touch with your own truth. Sovereignty begins when you start honoring the guidance that's already within you. This chapter invites you to quiet the outside world, reconnect to your inner compass, and remember that clear answers rise from your own stillness and not from consensus.

Reflect

Reflection invites you to witness where you've been deferring your power. If external seeking replaces inner trust, it creates disconnection from who you really are.

Notice how you've been giving your voice away, and why:

- When do you most often seek advice from others?
- What emotions are you avoiding by outsourcing decisions?

- What current decision in your life needs your own voice, not someone else's permission or opinion?

Journaling Prompt: *What am I truly seeking when I ask for advice and what part of me already knows the answer?*

Reframe

Advice can be helpful, but only if it serves your truth. You are here to live by conviction, not by committee.

- External input can offer perspective, but inner Sovereignty begins with self-trust.
- Reconnect with your core values. They are your soul's compass.
- Look back: What past decisions left you feeling proud, peaceful, or powerful?
  – What past decisions left you feeling proud, peaceful, or powerful?
  – What guided you then?
  – What can you reclaim from those moments now?

Empowering Thought: *Your clearest answers rise from within, not from consensus.*

Reconnect

Reconnection means hearing your own voice again. When you get quiet, what's true for you begins to surface. Sovereignty doesn't require loudness. It requires presence. Begin small, but begin within.

- **Create Intentional Space for Clarity**
  – Journal without filters.
  – Meditate with a single question in your heart.
  – Take long walks without your phone or distractions.

– Let quiet become your guide.
– Let your body respond before your mind intervenes.
– Notice the wisdom that arises
– Trust that the answers are already within you.

Affirmation: *I trust my inner wisdom. I make decisions from a place of clarity, love, and alignment. My truth lives within me.*

Final Thought: Your Wisdom Is the Loudest Voice When You Get Quiet

The answers you seek live within you.
Your wisdom waits beneath all noise.
Your knowing is steady, ancient, sure.
Your truth is always quietly present.

Stop chasing outside validation.
Start hearing your deeper truth.
Stop asking for permission.
Begin embodying your inner power.

Silence is sacred access, not emptiness.
Stillness is deep wisdom, not weakness.
Pause and listen with devotion.
Strengthen the bridge to intuition.

Clarity is something you allow.
Your next step always reveals itself.
You don't need more opinions.
You need fuller, deeper presence.

This is Sovereign Living.

PERCEPTION TO REALITY

"Perception is reality."
~ *Lee Atwater*

We often assume that truth speaks for itself. But the way others perceive us is their truth. This can be both empowering and frustrating.

We can influence how we're seen through how we show up. On the other hand, we are not always given the benefit of the doubt. People may judge based on their assumptions, projections, and misunderstandings.

Above all, Sovereignty means clear self-perception. When you live in Sovereignty, your inner reality begins to radiate outward. Over time, it even rewires how others see you.

My Story: Becoming the Woman Who Chooses Alignment Over Approval

I grew up in a beautifully diverse high school community, a vibrant mix of cultures, backgrounds, and beliefs. I was a cheerleader, dating the captain of the football team, and I also played basketball, moving easily between different circles. I prided myself on being warm and welcoming, believing that kindness could bridge any divide.

Then one night, someone made a comment about the company I kept, suggesting that my friends reflected who I was more than my actions did. His words unsettled me. I didn't agree with his judgment, but it planted a seed of awareness. For the first time, I began to see how perception and reality often blur, and how easily others can project their stories onto us.

That moment became a quiet teacher. I realized that staying true to myself wasn't just about being kind or openhearted, it was about being discerning with my energy. I learned that I could love people deeply without needing to align with every environment or behavior around me.

Today, I still consider myself a cheerleader at heart, someone who encourages, uplifts, and believes in others. But I've also learned to pause, reflect, and ask:

- Is this aligned with who I'm becoming?
- Am I showing up in a way that reflects my truth?
- Am I surrounding myself with energy that supports my growth?

Perception can be powerful, but reality is where peace lives. When your inner truth and outer world match, alignment replaces approval, and that's where Sovereignty begins.

Becoming the Woman You Already Are

Your self-perception is the foundation of your Sovereignty. It informs how you speak, move, lead, love, and live. But your identity can become distorted by others' assumptions or outdated roles. Sovereignty begins when you reclaim the authority to define yourself. This chapter invites you to stop performing and start embodying who you truly are.

Reflect

Who you believe yourself to be, consciously or unconsciously, influences every interaction, every boundary, every choice. Ask what stories you're still living by, and which ones you're ready to rewrite.

- How do you currently see yourself, in thought and in action?
- What do you genuinely love about how you present yourself in the world?
- What parts of you are ready to evolve into a higher expression?

Journaling Prompt: *Have I ever been misjudged? What did that experience teach me about expressing my truth and protecting my peace?*

Reframe

You are not here to be everything to everyone. You are here to be a living embodiment of your values and your vision. Your identity isn't fixed, it's evolving. Sovereignty is the conscious shaping of that process.

- You are not defined by others' assumptions. You are defined by your alignment.
- Instead of asking, "How am I being seen?" Ask, "How do I want others to feel in my presence?"
- Reframe your identity as a living expression of your values, your voice, and your soul's vision.

Empowering Question: *What version of myself am I ready to embody more consistently with clarity, confidence, and grace?*

Reconnect

Sovereignty thrives in reflections. Who are the people that reflect your highest truths, not your smallest fears. Choose those mirrors wisely. Choose to see yourself clearly.

- **Discern Your Circle**
  – Who mirrors your highest self? Who distorts it?
  – Express gratitude to those who uplift and empower you.
  – Create boundaries where energy is false, or constricting.

- **Fortify Yourself in Authenticity**
  – Allow your self-perception be shaped by your soul
  – Speak your truth.
  – Walk with presence.
  – Be the woman your younger self would admire.

Affirmation: *I define who I am. I live in truth, speak with grace, and align my perception with my soul's reality.*

Final Thought: Perception Begins With You

Perception begins within you.
Your energy sets the tone.
Your character shapes your path.
Your alignment leads the way.

Take full responsibility for yourself.
Own the space you occupy.
Stand tall in your truth.
Let the world catch up.

Adjust your circle boldly.
Evolve your habits intentionally.
Reintroduce yourself as you grow.
Choose what honors you.

Own your radiant light.
Live your deepest truth.
Trust your inner compass.
Your reality will follow.

This is Sovereign Living.

IDENTITY CRISIS TO IDENTITY CREATION

"Lose who you are perceived to be so you can become who you want to be."
~ *Matthew McConaughey*

What if the labels others have placed on you, titles, names, roles, are no longer accurate reflections of who you are?

Rebranding your identity isn't about pretending or performing. It's about stepping into your truth and becoming the author of your own story. Sovereignty means releasing who you've been so you can step fully into who you are and who you're becoming.

What would it look like to unbrand yourself, not for fame or recognition but for freedom to live more authentically?

My Story: Reclaiming My Name, Reclaiming My Self

After my divorce I kept my married name to honor my children's identity and to maintain the professional identity I'd built over 20 years. But when I moved to California something began to change.

During a deep meditation followed by a powerful breath work session, I heard my inner voice: *Take back your name and you will take back yourself.*

At first I resisted, but the message was unmistakable. I kept seeing the letter "A," the initial of my birth-given last name, drifting upward inside a single bubble. The image of the Vitruvian Man followed, his body rising into the shape of an A. It felt like a quiet reminder of who I am and where I come from, and in that moment I knew what I needed to do.

I filed for a legal name change. When the judge asked, "Why are you changing your name?" I replied, "I'm reclaiming my birth-given name, Laura Alfano."

It wasn't a rejection of the past. It was a declaration of who I am. Updating my identity across documents and platforms felt surprisingly ceremonial. I was no longer existing under someone else's karmic lineage. I was home in myself, in my name, and in my truth.

Reclaiming Your Identity

Over time, life assigns us names, roles, and labels. Some empower. Others confine. Sovereign identity begins when you stop living by default and start defining yourself. This chapter invites you to peel back layers of external expectation and return to who you were and who you are.

Reflect

What various identities have you worn? Which ones have you outgrown? To reclaim who you are, first acknowledge who you are not. Identity is not a fixed story. It's your soul's evolution.

- What labels, roles, or titles have shaped how others perceive you?
- Do those fit who you are becoming, or are they holding you back?

- What aspects of your present identity have you outgrown?

Journaling Prompt: *What have I outgrown and what within me is quietly asking to rise?*

Reframe

Reframing isn't about pretending to be someone new. It's removing what's no longer true so your real self can shine forth.

- You are not defined by who you've been. You are defined by who you *choose* to become.
- If you were to "rebrand" your identity today, what values and qualities would you lead with?
- This is not reinvention; it's a return. A remembering. A re-anchoring.

Empowering Thought: *Identity isn't fixed; it's a living expression of truth, clarity, and intention.*

Reconnect

The goal is not perfection. It's congruence. To show up in a way that feels true. The more you embody your essence, the less you need approval and the more your life reflects your Sovereignty.

- **Envision Your Fully Expressed Self**
  – What would it look and feel like to live as your boldest, most authentic self, starting now?
  – How would you walk?
  – What would you say yes to?
  – What would you release?

- **Radiate That Version of You Today**
  – Let your language reflect your new self.
  – Let your actions mirror your clarity.
  – Let your energy signal your change.
- You are not who the world says you are. You are who you choose to become.

Affirmation: *I am not who the world says I am. I am who I choose to become. I release outdated roles and reclaim my Sovereign identity, whole, bold, and free.*

Final Thought: Name It to Claim It

Your identity belongs to you.
Your name carries your truth.
No one else defines you.
Not family, not community, not the past.

You choose how you are known.
You choose what you answer to.
You choose the story you claim.
Your power begins there.

Stop asking for permission.
Stand fully in your becoming.
Let your presence speak clearly.
Let your truth rise unfiltered.

Rebranding is inner honoring.
It is choosing your next chapter.
It is meeting your truest self.
It is claiming the name that fits.

This is Sovereign Living.

JUDGMENT TO JUDGMENT DETOX

"Judgment is the number one reason we feel blocked, sad, and alone. Our culture places enormous value on social status, appearance, race, religion, and material wealth. We are made to feel less than, separate, and not good enough. To protect ourselves from feeling inadequate, insecure, or unworthy, we turn to judgment."
~ Gabrielle Bernstein

Judgment is the emotional shortcut your ego takes when you're too afraid to confront your own wounds. Judgment may offer a temporary high of superiority or control but it leaves a toxic residue.

We don't judge others because they're flawed. We judge because we haven't learned to lovingly meet the flawed parts of ourselves.

But you don't need to judge to protect your worth. You don't need to compete to prove your value. You are already whole.

My Story: Healing Through Forgiveness, Not Judgment

One of the most painful judgment moments of my life came during my divorce. In a small, close-knit town, word travels fast and opinions travel faster.

As soon as people learned I had initiated a divorce, the community split. Some supported me quietly. Others chose sides openly, aligning with my soon to be ex-husband.

Close friends who I had hosted in my home, people I supported through their own challenges and honored in their lives' milestones, suddenly turned cold, distant, and silent.

At first, I judged them right back. I created a mental list of betrayals. But that only made me feel more bitter, more isolated, and more alone.

I had to let go of judgment, mine and theirs. I turned to the practice Gabrielle Bernstein outlines in her book *Judgment Detox*. I began cutting the metaphorical energetic cords between me and the people whose judgments I feared.

Before attending my son's wedding, an event I had long dreamed of, I visualized each person I thought might judge me and released them in love. When the day arrived, I walked into the church radiant and free.

Most of those same friends who had rejected me, now embraced me with kindness. It wasn't because they had changed. It was because I had changed.

Clearing the Lens of the Heart

Judgment is a disguise, a shield we use to avoid deeper pain, insecurity, or disconnection. But it doesn't protect us. It separates us.

Sovereignty invites you to do the radical, tender work of choosing compassion. It's not because others deserve it. It's because you do.

Reflect

Reflection allows you to observe your judgments without shame. Judgment is a teacher if you're willing to listen. When you trace it back, you find a place in yourself that is still healing, still longing, or still afraid.

- Who have I recently judged, and why?
  Was it their success, appearance, lifestyle, beliefs, or behavior?

- What deeper emotion might be fueling that judgment?
  Jealousy, fear, rejection, comparison, feeling unseen?

- Whom do I feel judged by?
  How has that shaped my self-perception or behavior?

Journaling Prompt: *What is judgment trying to protect me from and what would it take to face that with love instead?*

Reframe

- Reframing invites you to soften your judgmental gaze. You can see yourself and others more clearly.
- What if judgment became a cue for compassion, toward others and toward yourself?
- What would shift if you viewed life through love instead of fear?

Empowering Thought: *Choosing compassion is not condoning behavior; it's freeing yourself from the burden of blame.*

Reconnect

Reconnection is the healing act of seeing through softer eyes, first inward and then outward. When you release judgment, you create space for empathy, intimacy, and grace to return. Start with yourself and go from there.

- **Practice Softening Your Gaze**
  – Pause when a judgmental thought arises.
  – What pain, fear, or need might this thought be masking?
  – Replace it with curiosity or understanding.

- **Forgive Yourself and Others**
  – Write a note of release.
  – Say aloud: "I release this story. I choose peace."

- **Start Small**
  – Replace one critical thought or comment with a compassionate one, even silently.
  – Notice how your energy shifts.

Affirmation: *I release judgment and choose compassion. I see myself and others through the eyes of love. I am free to heal.*

Final Thought: Judgment Is a Mirror, Not a Truth

Judgment never defines others.
It always reveals us.
It shows where love is missing.
It shows where love must flow.

Choose compassion over criticism.
Trade resistance for relief.
Release the need to be right.
Make room to be real.

Every harsh thought calls for healing.
Every softened gaze opens grace.
Blame cannot heal you.
Understanding always can.

Control cannot expand you.
Acceptance always will.
Let your heart be the mirror.
Let freedom begin with love.

This is Sovereign Living.

*"When we detox from judgment,
we reclaim our power to love."*
~ Laura Alfano

SEEKING HAPPINESS TO BEING HAPPINESS

*"If you want to live a
happy life, tie it to a goal,
not people or things."*
~ *Albert Einstein*

The suggestion that someone else can make you happy is one of the most disempowering myths we've been taught. We've been fed the idea that our joy depends on a partner, a paycheck, a job title, or a bigger house.

But happiness doesn't arrive in a package or in a person. It isn't something to be delivered or pursued. Happiness is something to become. It's cultivated in still moments, the mindful choices, and in the deep knowing that you are the source of your own joy.

My Story: A Note, a Trigger, and a Realization

A few years ago, after a relationship ended, I received a note from my former partner that read: "I'm sorry that I couldn't make you happier."

That struck a nerve, not because it was unkind, but because it missed the truth of who I had become.

I never expected someone to make me happy. What I expected was respect. I expected my boundaries to be honored. I expected peace in the quiet moments. Genuine companionship. A steady connection that felt alive but not overwhelming. His energy was restless, always moving, always anxious, never still. I felt it in my body and worked hard to keep my own nervous system calm and steady. What I truly wanted was something grounded and real, a relationship that moved at a natural pace, with space for both depth and ease.

Happiness, for me, has always been an inside job. It's shaped by the energy I bring into each day, how I care for myself, and the way I engage with the world around me. Of course, there are moments when I feel unhappy, but they're usually the result of crossed boundaries, not a lack of love or comfort.

I'm a generally happy person, and that's not by chance, it's by choice. Every morning and every night, I return to the same truth: I choose joy. I choose peace. I choose gratitude.

Becoming the Source of Your Joy

Too often we postpone happiness pending the next accomplishment, whether it's a promotion at work or a romantic partnership. Real joy lives in your ability to honor what's already good. This chapter invites you to stop chasing happiness and start embodying it from the inside out.

Reflect

Reflection is how you gently discover where you've been outsourcing your joy, placing it in someone else's hands or tying it to future outcomes. You don't need to judge those detours, just witness them. Then begin returning joy to its rightful place within you.

- Where are you still expecting someone or something to "make you happy"?

- Have you outsourced your joy to some future version of your life or yourself?
- When was the last time you felt truly happy? What was taking place at that moment?

Journaling Prompt: *What does happiness actually feel like in my body? Calm? Lightness? Energy? Playfulness?*

Reframe

Reframing helps you reclaim joy as an inside job. You don't need to earn it. You don't need to wait for it. It is available now through gratitude, intention, and presence. Your joy is not a product of perfection. It's a practice of perspective.

- Happiness isn't something to chase, it's something to choose and cultivate.
- Gratitude is the gateway. It anchors you in what's already beautiful.
- What small, present-moment joys already exist in your day. How can you invite more of them?
- Sometimes protecting your joy means protecting your peace. What boundaries need to be set, strengthened, or honored?

Empowering Thought: *You don't have to wait for happiness you can become the space that holds it.*

Reconnect

Reconnection is the act of practicing joy right now and right here. In real time. In your body. In your breath. In your laughter. The more you practice joy, the more your nervous system remembers it as home.

- **Practice Embodying Joy**
  – Savor a morning ritual: tea, light, music, stillness
  – Pause for simple gratitude: one breath or one thank you
  – Move your body with presence walk, stretch, dance. Let joy be in the "now," not in the "next."

- **Embody Joy as a Rhythm, Not a Reward**
  – You are not waiting for a reason.
  – You are choosing a rhythm that supports your wholeness.

Affirmation: *I am the source of my joy. I choose happiness. I radiate peace, gratitude, and love, because that is who I am.*

Final Thought: Happiness Is Your Birthright

Happiness is not found; it is remembered.
It has lived within you all along.
It waits for your awareness to return.
It rises when you finally look inward.

When you stop chasing joy, it arrives.
When you stop seeking approval, peace expands.
Happiness is not in the having.
It is always in the being.

It is quiet confidence in alignment.
It is the steady warmth of gratitude.
Joy is not earned through effort.
Joy is embodied through presence.

Each breath invites you home.
Each moment of gratitude opens light.
You are not searching for happiness.
You are remembering your radiant wholeness.

This is Sovereign Living.

BLIND TO SEEING

"Change the way you look at things, and the things you look at will change."
~ Dr. Wayne Dyer

We don't see the world as it is. We see it as we are.

We live in a hyper-stimulated world that rarely invites us to pause. We're trained to chase what's next, to react quickly, and to view challenges through the lens of inconvenience.

But every moment can be awesome when you're willing to shift your perspective. What was "boring," "ugly," or "stressful" can become beautiful, inspiring, and sacred. That shift doesn't require travel or luxury or a new home. It requires presence.

My Story: The Window Seat Shift

While attending a Wanderlust Yoga retreat in Sydney, Australia, I signed up for a class called The Art of Seeing. I needed rest, not another power flow.

Pete Longworth, our guide, was a fast-talking Aussie with soulful energy and a photographer's eye. In fact, he is a photographer. He encouraged us to consider life from fresh angles, even in frustrating places like airports and airplanes. "Always take the window seat," he said. "It's your portal to wonder."

Wow. I'd spent years rushing through airports, managing time, juggling work and family. Even on planes I was planning the next big thing. But Peter's advice slowed me down.

Now I always choose the window. I've seen cloud realms, sunsets that looked like fire, and skylines that reminded me how small we are. But more than that, I began to feel life again, not as a checklist but as moments waiting to be noticed.

I learned to reflect on what I was missing, reframe what I had called ordinary, and reconnect with a sense of awe.

Life's sacred moments often whisper, they don't shout. When your awareness softens, beauty reveals itself everywhere: in shadows, in silence, in small gestures.

Finding Beauty That Was Always There

Life's most sacred moments often whisper, they don't shout. But when your awareness softens, beauty begins to reveal itself everywhere: in shadows, in silence, in small gestures. This chapter invites you to trade distraction for devotion, and to find the extraordinary not by changing your life, but by seeing it differently.

Reflect

When you're overwhelmed, stressed, or chasing "something more," you miss the miracle of what already is..

- Where is your vision currently clouded? By stress or by routine? By expectation or by disappointment?
- When was the last time you noticed beauty in something ordinary? Light through a window, laughter, or a simple meal?

- What emotions or thoughts color how you see the world during challenging moments?
- Are you truly open to finding beauty even in discomfort or simplicity?

Journaling Prompt: *What area of my life feels dull or frustrating and how might I reframe it as sacred or beautiful?*

Reframe

Reframing invites you to shift your inner dialogue and change how you interpret your environment. Beauty is not reserved for perfect days. It lives in imperfection, in pause, in perspective. Wonder becomes available the moment you decide to meet the world with new eyes.

- Shift your perspective and let *wonder* replace weariness.
- **Try this new inner dialogue**
  – Instead of "This traffic is wasting my time," say: "This is an invitation to pause and breathe."
  – Instead of "Nothing special is happening," say: "Today is filled with moments I've never experienced before."
- Empower your perception by choosing a lens that honors presence and possibility.

Empowering Question: *How can I begin to see the sacred in what I've been overlooking?*

Reconnect

Reconnection means returning to the present with your body, your breath, and all your senses. Beauty doesn't hide. It waits to be seen. When you tune into the details of life, even the mundane becomes meaningful.

- **Practice Open-Eye Meditation**
  Wherever you are, car, kitchen, desk, garden:
  – Take a slow, grounding breath
  – Gently scan your space
  – Let your eyes rest on one detail
  – Observe it deeply. Let it tell a story.
  – Ask Yourself: "What is this moment awakening in me?"

- **Create Beauty Awareness Prompts**
  – What are three "window seat" moments to create this week?
  – Where can you soften your gaze and see with new eyes?
  – What would shift if you treated ordinary moments like sacred invitations?

Affirmation: *I choose to see clearly. I soften into the present moment. Beauty surrounds me, because I choose to see it.*

Final Thought: Seeing Is a Soul Skill

True sight begins in stillness.
It begins when the heart opens.
Your eyes do not fail you.
Your pace simply moves too fast.

Slow down and colors return.
Pause and beauty steps forward.
Seeing is presence, not effort.
Attention is its sacred doorway.

Soften your gaze gently.
Let shadows reveal their stories.
Breathe and the ordinary becomes holy.
Every detail becomes an invitation.

You don't need a new view.
You need a new way of looking.
See with your soul's reverence.
Awaken to the grace already here.

This is Sovereign Living.

WEARING CLOTHES TO CURATING A SIGNATURE LOOK

"Dress shabbily, and they remember the dress; dress impeccably, and they remember the woman."
~ *Coco Chanel*

We are always communicating one way or another. Clothing, for instance, is a visual language. It signals who you are and how you feel. Sovereign women don't dress to impress. They dress to express themselves.

Cinema has shown us this truth again and again. In *The Devil Wears Prada*, Andy's transformation walk is not about designer labels, but about stepping into a more confident, intentional version of herself. The clothes simply reflected the woman who was ready to be seen. And in *Pretty Woman*, Vivian's red opera gown doesn't make her worthy; it reveals the worth that had been there all along. These moments remind us that when your outer expression aligns with your inner becoming, you don't just look different, you lead differently.

Your wardrobe can either mute your presence or amplify your essence. The shift happens when you stop dressing for approval and start dressing in alignment with your inner authority.

My Story: Wearing Confidence Like a Second Skin

Growing up in a proud Italian immigrant household, the right appearance was essential. My father, a barber by trade, believed that how you dressed said everything about your self-respect. Before dinner, my siblings and I were scrubbed, coiffed, and polished like a showroom-ready new car. If I emerged in anything deemed sloppy or too revealing, I'd hear, "Go back and try again. You are what you wear."

By my twenties, I had mastered the art of balancing elegance with strength. A degree in fashion merchandising, paired with a deep fascination for New York City's dynamic fashion scene taught me the nuances of trend interpretation. Thank you Carolina Herrara, Norma Kamali, Donna Karan and Betsey Johnson.

My experience working part time at Neiman Marcus opened the doors to the world of luxury styling and timeless brands, such as Louis Vuitton, Chanel and Gucci. Fashion was evolving beyond self-expression to become a form of identity and self-possession.

Today, at 61 years old and living in Southern California, my style is effortless but intentional. I wear long, flowing fabrics, dresses and jumpsuits. Palettes are neutral with the occasional pop of soft pink or a wild card like leopard print. Everything I wear is designed for movement, for ease, for presence. Never dressing to please others, I always dress to feel like the woman I am and the one I'm still becoming.

Curating your signature look is not about shopping. It is about Sovereignty. It is about claiming how you want to be seen and how you choose to move through the world. One of my favorite memories with my youngest daughter taught me just how early this awareness begins to take shape.

One Saturday after a lacrosse game, I took her and a few friends to Subway for a quick bite. They were disheveled from the field, still in their pinnies, headbands, high socks, and slip-on sandals. We lived in a cluster of small towns, and it happened to be prom season. The girls were excited about the idea of asking boys from another school.

As we walked in, a group of lacrosse boys from a nearby town were already there. The girls froze. In an instant, their confidence evaporated. They no longer saw themselves as strong young athletes who had just played their hearts out, but as "not enough" in messy hair and post-game clothes.

"How could we possibly talk to anyone looking like this?" one whispered. I encouraged them to see beyond the surface, to trust that who they were mattered more than what they wore. But their discomfort spoke louder than my reassurance. We took our sandwiches to go.

In that moment, something rose in me, a teaching I didn't plan but one that stayed with all of us. "Girls," I said, "from this day forward, be prom ready when you leave the house." They blinked, confused. "What does that mean?"

"It means taking a moment," I said. "Asking yourself, If I meet someone new today, is this the impression I want to leave? Not to impress others, but to honor yourself. To show up as the young woman you aspire to be, not the one shrinking from being seen."

A soft "ohhh" filled the car. It was never about perfection. It was always about presence.

Years later, more than just that original group uses the expression. They carry it into interviews, auditions, first dates, and coffee shops. And whenever they share a story about meeting someone new, I always ask, "Were you prom ready?"

When they weren't, they laugh and admit they wished they had been, because they understand now what they didn't then: "Prom ready" was never about makeup or matching outfits. It was about Sovereignty. It was about showing up with intention, dressing for the woman they were becoming rather than the fear that made them hide. That is the heart of a signature style. It is a daily act of self-respect, a quiet and powerful declaration that says, I am worthy of being seen.

Style as a Statement of Sovereignty

Style isn't shallow, it's soulful. What you wear tells the world who you are, what you value, and how you carry your power. Your appearance shouldn't be about conformity or consumption. It's about clarity. Step into your closet to curate your expression and to wear your worth boldly and beautifully.

Reflect

Reflection helps you examine the unconscious ways you've been dressing for acceptance, comfort, or invisibility. Reflection invites you to shift toward expression, alignment, and expansion. Your clothes tell a story. What story are they telling?

- When you look in the mirror, do you see a woman who reflects your inner essence?

- Does your wardrobe support or suppress the version you're stepping into?
- When do you feel most alive in your clothing? When do you tend to hide?

Journaling Prompts: *What three words do I want my appearance to communicate? What pieces in my current wardrobe reflect who I am becoming? How do I want to feel when I get dressed?*

Reframe

Treat style not as vanity, but as a vehicle of visibility. When you dress with intention, you embody your energy before you speak. Style becomes a sacred ritual, an external sign of your inner evolution.

- Style is power in motion.
- Your signature look is an outward affirmation of internal truth.
- Getting dressed should be a ritual of identity and intention.
- Your clothes can mute you or amplify you. Choose to be amplified.

Empowering Thought: *Style isn't about impressing others. It's about expressing yourself with clarity, confidence, and grace.*

Reconnect

Fashion reconnection means expressing yourself boldly, consciously, and creatively. It isn't about trend-chasing, it's about truth-wearing. When your external reflection embodies your internal, alignment deepens, and the world begins to recognize your presence before you speak.

- **Start Small, Start Strong**
  Choose one intentional outfit this week that reflects your future self. Ask: "Does this express who I am becoming?"

- **Choose a Power Piece**
  – A fitted blazer, a bold lipstick color, a silky scarf, a necklace, something that feels like your Crown.
  – Let it anchor your energy and elevate your presence.

- **Create a "Look & Feel" Board**
  – Use Pinterest, a journal, or a wall collage to gather visual inspiration.
  – Use references that reflect your energy, not just your body.
  – Follow a fashion brand on Instagram that reflects your aspirational style, and when needed, seek out a more accessible piece that offers the same feeling and expression.

- **Mirror Practice**
  – Stand in front of the mirror. Hold your gaze.
  – Ask Yourself: "Do I look like someone who knows her worth?"

Affirmation: *I wear my truth. I move with grace. I embody my power with one look, one choice, one day at a time.*

Final Thought: You're Not Just Getting Dressed; You're Getting Ready to Lead

Style is consciousness expressed beautifully.
Your energy speaks first.
Your presence arrives before words.
Every outfit tells a story.

Every detail whispers becoming.
Dress with deep intention.
Align your inner and outer worlds.
Curate your presence with care.

This is not fashion.
This is frequency embodied.
Wear what honors your becoming.
Let your look reflect your truth.

Your wardrobe is your sanctuary.
Each piece is a declaration.
Walk as the woman you are.
Dress to lead your life.

This is Sovereign Living.

Part Three

MANIFESTATION
IGNITE YOUR DREAMS, ALIGN YOUR PATH & EMBODY YOUR DESTINY

Manifestation is not about forcing outcomes but aligning with divine rhythm. It is the art of creation through consciousness, where thought becomes form and intention becomes movement. The dreamer becomes the architect, the seeker becomes the source, and the unseen becomes the seen.

In **Manifesting from Neptune in Pisces to Neptune in Aries**, you step from dreaming to doing, from intuition to inspired action. The era of vision meets the fire of embodiment, where imagination becomes momentum. **Limited Beliefs to Limitless Possibilities** invites you to break free from patterns of lack, expanding your sense of what is possible when you believe you are worthy of more.

Through **Dreamer to Doer**, you move from intention to implementation, learning that manifestation is not magic without movement but energy guided by purpose. **Wandering to Wanderlust** rekindles curiosity and adventure, reminding you that expansion requires exploration, both inner and outer.

In **Perfection to Passion**, you release control and rediscover creativity as play, allowing expression to lead the way. **Loss to Gratitude** transforms pain into wisdom, teaching that endings are portals and gratitude is the frequency that attracts grace.

Scarcity to Abundance opens the gates to prosperity consciousness. You learn that wealth begins in thought, expands through generosity, and flows where faith is present. In **Cluttered Mind to Laser-Focused Desire**, you clear mental noise to make space for divine direction, realizing that clarity is the currency of creation.

Distraction to Intentional Action reminds you that focus is sacred. Every choice and moment becomes a prayer of purpose. Through **Obsession with an Idea to Planting the Seed of Desire**, you learn the difference between clinging and cultivating. You plant intentions in alignment, then release control and let the universe conspire.

In **Resistance to Persistence**, you meet the devotion that sustains creation. True manifestation is born not of urgency but of trust. **Bird's Eye View to Spy Plane View** invites you to rise above daily distractions and view your life from a higher perspective, one guided by clarity, strategy, and purpose. From this elevated vantage point, you stop reacting to circumstances and begin intentionally designing your future, aligning every choice with vision, values, and calm discernment. **Pessimism to Optimism** reframes doubt as faith in motion, while *No to a Resounding Yes!* becomes your anthem of courage, a reminder that saying *yes* to your soul can change everything.

Finally, **Release to Expand** teaches that letting go is not loss but liberation. Surrender becomes your superpower, opening space for grace to flow.

Manifestation is the royal art of co-creation with life itself, graceful, grounded, and guided by love.

MANIFESTING FROM NEPTUNE IN PISCES TO NEPTUNE IN ARIES

"The secret of getting ahead is getting started."
~ *Mark Twain*

The entry of Neptune into Aries on March 30, 2025 marked one of the most profound astrological shifts of our lifetime. Neptune, the planet of dreams, spirituality, and intuition, had not entered Aries for 165 years.

This rare event is the beginning of a new 165-year cycle around the Sun. The final sign of the zodiac stepping into the first signals a rebirth collectively and individually. A portal is opening: from unity and dissolution into bold self-Sovereignty.

In Pisces, Neptune expressed itself through collective consciousness, compassion, and spiritual oneness. It was a season of surrender, of dissolving into the whole. As Neptune moves into Aries, the energy pivots toward assertive individuality, leadership, and action.

On a personal level, we will shift from passive observation to active creation. We are no longer relying on blind faith. We are called to become the hero of our own journeys, boldly initiating the dreams we once only imagined.

Nations, communities, and individuals are now reclaiming their unique identities. Borders will be redrawn not only geographically, but spiritually and culturally.

Neptune in Aries invites a renaissance of tradition, not from nostalgia but from fierce self-ownership. We'll see this in the arts, technology, spirituality, and everywhere that authenticity triumphs over mass conformity.

This transit also promises profound exploration into outer space, the oceans, and the depths of human consciousness. Expect a rise in decentralized systems, off-grid living, DIY cultures, and Sovereign communities, all fueled by a hunger for independence from outdated structures.

Fortunately, Neptune in Aries will align harmoniously with Pluto in Aquarius and Uranus in Gemini in the years ahead. This mandates that innovation, collaboration, and visionary leadership will pave the way for positive transformation.

My Story: Turning Dreams into Action

Learning that Neptune had moved into Aries was like a bell ringing in my soul. I could feel the truth of it, not just astrologically but somatically. I had already begun moving out of the dreamscape of the past decade and into something sharper and more alive. I was ready to act.

In my work, I've always moved between spiritual insight and practical action. During Neptune in Pisces, much of my visioning lived in the ethereal. Beautiful, moving, and true. But at times it lacked manifestation.

Now, I feel a fire returning. The dreams I once wrote quietly in journals are becoming outlines. Proposals. Projects. Conversations. I'm stepping forward to be of service to others.

I joined a new real estate agency, built out a luxury real estate website, took another trip to Italy, spent time with the people I love and after 9 years finished my book, which turned out to be three.

Aries doesn't whisper. It moves. It leads. It says *yes!* Not just to the dream, but to the discipline that will make it real. This next era, for me, is about embodiment. About being less "in potential" and more "in purpose."

Neptune in Aries isn't about waiting for the stars to align. It's about realizing the stars already live inside you and then choosing to rise.

Igniting Desire into Action

Aries energy is bold, unapologetic, and instinct-driven. It doesn't wait for permission, it moves. This chapter invites you to activate your desires with the fire of Aries energy through clarity, courage, and aligned action. No more waiting for the right time. Now is sacred. Now is Sovereign.

Reflect

Reflection invites you to locate the dreams you've placed on the back burner. Dreams you told yourself you'll pursue when you're more ready, more qualified, more sure. But true creation doesn't begin with certainty. It begins with desire and decision. Desire is the divine spark of decision. Are you honoring it or hiding it?

- What dreams or desires have you delayed, waiting for timing, approval, or proof?
- Where have you been hoping life will shift instead of consciously shaping it?
- When you think about full ownership of your path, your time, your power and your destiny, do you feel fear or freedom?

Journaling Prompt: *What have I been waiting to begin? How would it feel to stop waiting?*

Reframe

Manifestation is not a wish. It's a willingness to trust your inspiration. To act before you're certain. To move before you're validated. Aries energy initiates. Your deepest desires don't need perfection. They need motion.

- You are not unprepared. You are in progress. You are becoming.
- Manifestation means engagement. It's showing up. It's doing the next brave thing.
- Readiness is not a prerequisite. You don't need to feel ready. You need to get started.

Mantra: *I manifest through movement. My soul leads. I follow.*

Reconnect

Aries charges forward. Its energy reminds you that every step is a sacred flame. Self-initiation is your birthright. Action aligns your internal fire with external form.

- **Name Your Desire Out Loud**
  Write it down. Speak it. Claim the dream you've been whispering inside. Let it echo outside of you.

- **Take One Tangible Step Make the call**
  – Sign up for the class.
  – Send the email.
  – Invest. Inquire. Initiate.

- **Start a Morning Mantra Practice**
  Each day, say: "I manifest through movement. My soul leads. I follow."

- **Celebrate Progress, Not Perfection**
  Every step is momentum. Every action is an offering. Aries reminds you: forward is enough.

Affirmation: *I was born to begin. I was born to blaze. My dreams are divine and I move with purpose.*

Final Thought: Ignite the Dream

Neptune in Aries is ignition.
Your dream is ready now.
You have healed enough.
You have grown enough.

This is your moment.
Rise into your becoming.
Become the artist.
Become the architect.

Become the leader.
Become the healer.
Move from vision to action.
Let purpose light your path.

The world needs your fire.
Strike your inner match.
Walk forward with soul.
Create with full Sovereignty.

This is Sovereign Living.

LIMITED BELIEFS TO LIMITLESS POSSIBILITIES

"We all get what we tolerate. Stop tolerating excuses within yourself, limiting beliefs of the past, or half-assed fearful states."
~ Tony Robbins

At some point early in life someone we loved and trusted may have unknowingly passed on a limiting belief. It might have sounded like:

"You have to work hard for money."

"One day you'll get married and have kids."

"The rich get richer, and the poor get poorer."

These phrases, innocently offered, can take root in our subconscious, quietly shaping how we view ourselves, our potential, and the world around us. Over time they form an invisible framework of our choices, actions, and self-worth.

Limiting beliefs are not just thoughts. They are inherited narratives and inherited fears disguised as truths.

But they are not permanent. We are not required to live by them. We are invited to outgrow them.

My Story: From Rebellion to Sovereignty

As a child, I was often labeled as "Too much. Too energetic. Too stubborn. Too defiant."

What others saw as rebellion, I now recognize as an early instinct for Sovereignty. I wasn't trying to be difficult. I was trying to be the truest version of myself. Even before I had the words for it, I could feel when someone else's rules didn't fit my truth. And I pushed back.

I had a knowing inside me that there is more than one way to live, love, work, and succeed, and that knowing stayed with me. It helped me question tradition when it felt like a trap. It helped me redefine success, love, and even motherhood on my own terms.

I still carry some limiting beliefs. We all do. But now I see them as invitations to expand.

Every time I challenge a limitation, I step further into my own truth. That truth says: You are not here to fit in a mold. You are here to break the mold and build something beautiful.

Freeing Yourself From the Limits You Inherited

Possibility begins where old beliefs end. Many perceptions are not personal truths. They are inherited scripts, shaped by fear, culture, or conditioning. So question what you've accepted, rewrite what you've been told, and awaken to the truth. The life you crave is possible and it starts with what you believe.

Reflect

Reflection is where liberation starts. Before you expand, you must reflect on the stories that have shaped your sense of what's possible. When you pause and find the script that's holding you back, you gain the power to rewrite it.

- What beliefs did you inherit about success, love, money, creativity, or worth? Start to question them.
- Whose voice echoes in your mind when you second-guess yourself?
- Where do you feel stuck right now? What belief keeps you there?

Journaling Prompt: *What have I believed about myself that no longer feels true and what am I ready to believe instead?*

Reframe

Reframing gives you the freedom to choose again. What you inherited isn't what you have to keep. Every belief is a doorway. You can choose whether to walk through it or build a new one. If someone else has done what you dream of, it means the path exists. If no one has, it means you are the pioneer. Say:

- "This isn't my belief, it was handed to me. I can choose a new one."
- "If someone has done what I dream of doing, it means I can too."
- "My potential is far greater than the limits I've been taught to accept."

Mantra: *I am not bound by belief. I choose what expands me.*

Reconnect

Reconnection is the practice of building your life by intentionally choosing new beliefs, embodying them. You surround yourself with mirrors that reflect your possibilities, not your limitations.

- **Rewrite the Story**
  Identify one limiting belief. Then replace it with a liberating truth:
  – Limiting: "I was not meant to lead."
  – Liberating: "I was born to rise and guide from my heart."

- **Speak It Daily**
  Say your new belief out loud each morning. Speak it like a vow. Let your body feel it.

- **Surround Yourself With Possibility**
  Seek mentors, communities, and friendships that stretch you. Be around those who live in expansion not fear.

- **Follow the Evidence**
  Find stories of people who've defied their past, their doubt, their odds. Let their courage ignite your own.

Affirmation: *I release the beliefs that confined me. I step into a life defined by truth, courage, and limitless possibility.*

Final Thought: You Are Not Here to Shrink

You are not too late.
You are not too old.
You are not too much.
You are right on time.

You are here to expand.
You are here to rise.
You are here to unfold.
You are here to become.

Challenge what you were told.
Question what was passed down.
Believe in your own truth.
Honor your inner knowing.

You change more than your life.
You change your lineage.
This is your revolution.
And you are ready now.

This is Sovereign Living.

DREAMER TO DOER

"Dreams are lovely, but they are just dreams. Dreams don't come true because you dream them. It's hard work that creates change."
~ *Shonda Rhimes*

Dreams are sacred. They ignite the heart, awaken the spirit, and whisper possibilities into the quiet corners of your mind. But without action, they stay in the realm of "someday."

In her unforgettable commencement speech at Dartmouth, Shonda Rhimes issued a bold truth: "Ditch the dream. Be a doer, not just a dreamer."

You don't need to wait for clarity. You don't need a perfect plan. You simply need to begin. Momentum comes from moving.

My Story: From Dream to Destiny

I've had the visionary mind of a dreamer, thanks to my sun sign, Libra, an Air sign, and the bold drive of a doer from my rising sign of Aries, a Fire sign.

When I was younger, my dreams were practical and heartfelt: a stable home, a family, and a good life. But I still knew something deeper within me was whispering. That whisper became louder over time.

One of those quiet dreams was to become a realtor. I've always known that a home is sacred space, and helping others find one was like a divine calling.

While living in Conneticut, I began taking some steps. I studied the markets. I surrounded myself with people in the industry. I said yes to opportunities that looked like side doors but were actually front gates. I pursued yoga teacher training and real estate licensing at the same time. One for the soul, one for the dream.

Shortly after, I moved to California and passed my state exam. Now I practice real estate in one of the most iconic markets in the world, Malibu.

There was no grand plan. Just action. And action became alignment. And alignment became arrival.

Someday Is Now

Dreams are not meant to remain in the realm of imagination. They are meant to be lived. Too often we confuse preparation with progress. We wait for permission but we can only give that to ourselves. You need to stop circling your calling and start walking toward it. Boldly. Imperfectly. Now.

Reflect

Reflection means re-naming the dreams you've called "timing" or "readiness." Sometimes what holds us back isn't fear of failure, it's fear of finally beginning.

- What vision or desire have you carried in your heart for years, even decades?

- Have you been mistaking research, planning, or talking about the dream as progress without taking real action?
- Where are you still waiting for someone else's validation or approval?

Journaling Prompt: *What dream keeps calling me and what has kept me from answering until now?*

Reframe

Reframing invites you to see that you are not late, now you're aligned. You're not unprepared, now you're in motion. Dreams are made real not by perfect timing, but by consistent action. Readiness is not a feeling. It's a decision to begin ready or not.

- You're not behind. You're on the edge of a breakthrough.
- It isn't about being ready. It's about being willing.
- One small action today is worth more than a perfect plan tomorrow.

Mantra: *I move forward, not because I have it all figured out, but because I refuse to wait any longer.*

Reconnect

Reconnection is the sacred act of aligning your values with your calendar. Dreams manifest not through old hopes but through new habits. The shift happens when you stop saying "someday" and start building something today.

- **Choose One Dream You've Delayed**
  Name it. Honor it. No matter how big or far off it feels, choose this as your starting point.

- **Write Down Why It Matters**
  Why is this dream important to you? What will it unlock? Who might it impact beyond yourself?

- **Schedule the Very Next Step**
  – Enroll in the class. Send the email. Research the next step.
  – Make time to write, record, build, and move.

- **Speak It Aloud**
  Stand tall and say: "I am doing this not someday, but now." Let your body believe it. Let your spirit respond.

Affirmation: *I no longer wait for the perfect moment. I act on what matters. My dreams move through me into the world now.*

Final Thought: Be the Doer Your Dream Deserves

Dreams are meant to be lived.
Dreams are meant to stretch you.
Dreams are meant to stir you.
Dreams are meant to move you.

Your dream is asking for movement.
It is not asking perfection.
It is asking for action.
It is asking for courage.

Even messy steps matter.
Even unsure steps count.
The future favors the bold.
Momentum changes everything.

Step before the path clears.
Start now, without delay.
Do the thing bravely.
Be the one your dream deserves.

This is Sovereign Living.

Pro Tip:
How to know your sun, moon or rising signs? Go to AstrologyCafe.com for your free natal chart report. All you need is your date of birth, time of birth and place of birth (city, state, country).

WANDERING TO WANDERLUST

"Not all who wander are lost"
~ J.R.R. Tolkien

There comes a time when wandering is no longer aimless. It becomes intentional. It becomes a calling from your soul, inviting you to pause, step away, and reimagine what a fulfilling life could look like beyond the path you were handed or the expectations you silently accept or self-imposed.

This kind of wandering isn't running away. It is a Soulbbatical, a term coined by Shelley Paxton, author of *Soulbbatical: A Corporate Rebel's Guide to Finding Your Best Life*, inviting you to become the Chief Soul Officer of your own life, a sacred journey inward.

Taking a Soulbbatical, even for just a few days or weeks, is a radical act of self-trust and self-honor. It's not about escape; it's about remembering who you are when the noise fades. For me, Soulbbaticals have become more than occasional getaways. They are a way of living. A rhythm of return to my most aligned, awake, and alive self.

My Story: From Sun-Soaked Beaches to Inner Exploration

For years, a vacation meant a warm-weather destination.
- An ocean view.
- A blanket on the sand.
- No agenda.

- Just breathing.
- Sun-soaking.
- Letting the waves do their quiet work of restoration.

My childhood and subsequently my children's, were seaside summers: swimming, climbing lifeguard towers, sandwiches, ice cream and fireworks with cousins.

But everything changed in the summer of 2014, just before I turned 50.

That year, my soul-seeking sister Kimberly invited me to my first Wanderlust Yoga Festival in Stratton, Vermont. What began as a getaway turned into a gateway, the start of a new kind of travel. It didn't just recharge my body. It rekindled my spirit.

Since then, my Soulbbatical path has expanded across the world:

- Yoga retreats around the world, from NY to Vermont to Italy to Sydney, to Bali with soul sister Kimberly.
- A transformative week with Chip Conley at Modern Elder Academy in Baja.
- A birthday weekend with my cousin-sister Lu at Oprah's *Live Your Best Life* Tour, where I met Rob Bell and Elizabeth Gilbert for the first time.
- A Sacred pilgrimages through Italy's churches and my father's birthplace.
- A life-changing plant medicine journey with my daughter Maddie at Rythmia Life Advancement Center in Costa Rica.

These wanderings became a weaving of memory, meaning, and medicine.

You don't have to write a book or quit your job to follow your soul. You simply have to start listening.

Take the Sacred Journey Back to You

The most transformative journeys don't always require a passport. A sacred pause, an intentional day, or even an afternoon alone can reconnect you to your essence. You step away from productivity long enough to remember who you are beneath the noise. This is your permission to wander, not to escape, but to return to yourself.

Reflect

Reflection means checking in with the part of you that doesn't speak in tasks or to-do lists. When was the last time you traveled not outward, but inward? Often what you crave most isn't more stimulation, but space to feel, to dream, and to hear your own inner voice again.

- What does your soul need most right now: stillness, adventure, reconnection, or reimagination?
- When was the last time you traveled or took space with no agenda other than to feel more like yourself?
- Have you allowed yourself the kind of pause that nourishes your spirit, not just your schedule?

Journaling Prompt: *What part of me is longing to be heard and what kind of journey will help me hear it?*

Reframe

Reframing reminds you that intentional solitude is sacred. In a world that praises output, creating time to be with your own being is an act of power.

- You don't need a major trip. You need a soul-led moment that says: "This is for me. This is for now."
- You don't need a plane ticket or a month-long escape. You need an intentional pause.
- "Wandering" isn't being lost, it's being open. Open to stillness. Open to clarity. Open to rediscovery.

Mantra: *I don't need to escape my life. I just need to return to myself.*

Reconnect

Reconnection is about giving your soul the space it's been whispering for. Whether it's an afternoon in nature, a solo retreat, or a silent morning by candlelight, these pauses restore your inner compass. You don't have to go far to come home to yourself.

- **Create a Wanderlust fund**
  – Open a small savings account or envelope.
  – Contribute consistently, even if it's $5/week.
  – Intention builds momentum.

- **Choose a Local Escape**
  Book a retreat, attend a workshop, visit a museum solo, or spend a night alone in nature or a quiet Airbnb.

- **Walk, Wander, and Listen**
  Take your journal and go somewhere new: a forest trail, a riverside, an overlook. Let your environment speak. Let your soul respond.

- **Treat Time With Yourself as Sacred**
  Light a candle. Brew tea slowly. Journal with presence. Let your rituals remind you: I am worthy of this time.

Affirmation: *I travel within to remember who I am. My presence is my power. My soul leads me home.*

Final Thought: Wander With Purpose

You are not lost, only unfolding.
You are becoming something truer.
Every wander carries quiet wisdom.
Every step brings you homeward.

Return to your deepest essence.
Return to your original truth.
Return to your bright aliveness.
Return to your inner center.

You don't need a crisis.
You only need permission.
Give yourself the sacred yes.
Go where your soul calls.

Sit gently with the sky.
Let the land steady you.
Let the silence hold you.
Run toward your next self.

This is Sovereign Living.

Pro Tip:
Need a nudge?

Read the book *Soulbbatical: A Corporate Rebel's Guide to Finding Your Best Life* by Shelly Paxton.

It's an invitation to become the Chief Soul Officer of your own life.

Fair warning: it might just change everything.

Additional warning: Read with a box of tissues.

PERFECTION TO PASSION

"Passion drives perfection."
~ Rick Warren

There's a profound difference between living a life fueled by passion and a life that demands perfection.

Passion is alive, creative, expansive. It allows room for mistakes, growth, and serendipity. It calls you forward even when the outcome is uncertain. It asks for your full presence.

Perfection, promises admiration but delivers anxiety. It seeks control where spontaneity is needed. It may seem beautiful on the surface, but it disconnects us from deeper selves and from others in the process.

When you choose passion over perfection, you return to your truth. You allow the messy, magnificent parts of life to take the lead. You release something more important than approval. You unlock joy.

My Story: From Polished to Purposeful

I became the Marketing Director for a yoga retreat center in Costa Rica. I saw it as a perfect alignment of spirituality, professional success, and tropical beauty.

My first major event was sponsored by Yoga Journal in Fort Lauderdale. I showed up proudly in branded yoga apparel that I had custom-made. The logo perfectly placed across my chest and down one leg. Everything was organized, well-planned, and on-brand. I looked the part.

But something deeper stirred below the surface. The turning point came unexpectedly during a keynote by Danielle LaPorte, author of *The Desire Map*. Her presence was electric, her words both fierce and tender.

During the Q&A, a woman stood up beside her grown daughter and said in a trembling voice, "I've spent my whole life being what everyone needs, a daughter, a wife, a mother. Now I don't know who I am. I have no desires"

The room went still until Danielle suggested this: "What if new desires are just waiting for you to claim them? Then you can begin again. "

I felt something open in me. It was an invitation to help mature women answer a persistent question in their lives: "What now?"

I asked some questions of myself:

- What do I want, not what's expected of me?
- What brings me alive, beyond performance or perfectionism?
- How do I want to live this next stage of my life?
- What is the path to closing the gap?

The next day I pulled a card from Danielle's "Truthbomb" inspirational card deck at her workshop.

The card read, "Passion Over Perfection."

The synchronicity was undeniable. I placed that card in my bathroom so I would look at it every day. It became a quiet declaration: I choose passion. I choose presence. I choose progress over polish.

Keep the Flame of Passion Burning without Burning Out

Passion is sacred fuel. But without boundaries it can become a wildfire. People burn out when they chase perfection or approval instead of honoring flow. Keep your fire alive with presence, not pressure. You don't need to be flawless to make a difference. You just need to stay lit from within.

Reflect

Reflection invites you to notice where your passion may have been replaced by performance. Are you showing up with soul, or trying to control how you're seen? Rather than perfection, passion demands the kind of permission that comes from you, not others.

- Where in your life are you clinging to perfection out of fear of judgment, failure, or being "not enough"?
- What passion, idea, or creative spark would you begin today if you didn't feel the need to do it flawlessly?
- When was the last time you felt fully lit up by something and what stopped you from following that feeling?

Journaling Prompt: *What would I dare to begin if I let myself be messy, honest, and fully alive?*

Reframe

- Passion-based mistakes don't mean you're off track. They're signs you're moving. You don't have to be perfect to be powerful. You have to be true.
- Passion isn't sloppy, it's sincere. It's your soul in motion.
- Your impact doesn't come from how polished you are. It comes from how present you are.

Mantra: *My fire doesn't need to be perfect. It just needs to be real.*

Reconnect

Reconnection is the practice of choosing aligned action over delayed perfection. Passion lives small steps, shared sparks, honest expression. Take care of your inner fire. Tend it with joy, not pressure. Let it warm others without consuming yourself.

- **Write Down Three Things That Light You Up**
  Think of what makes you feel alive, even if it scares you. Especially if it scares you.
- **Take One Brave Step Toward One of Them**
  – Make the call.
  – Sign up for the class.
  – Write the first page.
  – Speak the idea aloud.
- **Let Yourself Be Seen**
  Share your passion with someone you trust. Not your resume. Your real version. Let them see the spark, not the script.

Affirmation: *I tend to my fire with care. I move with joy, not pressure. My passion is my power and it lights the way.*

Final Thought: Lead With Heart, Not Haste

Perfection may win applause.
Passion builds true legacies.
Let your heart lead bravely.
Let your voice tremble forward.

Let your joy guide you.
Let your hands shake anyway.
You are not here to impress.
You are here to express.

Don't wait for perfect order.
Begin before you're ready.
Begin beautifully messy.
Begin boldly today.

The world needs your passion.
The world needs your presence.
The world needs your truth.
Lead with heart, not haste.

This is Sovereign Living.

LOSS TO GRATITUDE

"The more we give thanks, the more we receive to be thankful for. Gratitude is the gift that always gives back."
~ Matthew McConaughey

Matthew McConaughey stood on the Oscar stage before 43 million viewers and said, "Gratitude reciprocates." That wasn't just a heartfelt phrase. It was a cosmic and scientific truth.

Gratitude doesn't just make you feel better. It even makes you physically better. Dr. Robert Emmons, a leading researcher at UC Davis, found that people who consistently practice gratitude experience:

- Higher energy levels
- Better sleep
- Stronger emotional resilience
- Greater measurable progress toward goals

Gratitude strengthens relationships, helps you savor life's best moments, and allows you to transform adversity into wisdom. It's not just an emotion. It's a superpower.

Transforming Loss into Gratitude

Gratitude becomes even more profound when paired with grief.

Loss is universal. We all lose people, places, dreams, or seasons of life. But gratitude gives you a new lens that honors what was received, not just what was lost.

Instead of asking, "Why did this happen to me?" gratitude invites the question, "What was the gift?"

It's the practice of transforming pain into presence, heartbreak into hope, and endings into beginnings.

My Story: Becoming Still and Grateful

When my brother died, I coped by doing.

I organized everything: his funeral service, our family logistics, and the unspoken emotional load.

I didn't pause. I didn't feel it because I couldn't afford to. I was raising a family. I was keeping up with children's homework, managing two homes, three cars and working full time.

Twelve years later my father passed. While I still organized the immediate needs, when it was over I made a different choice.

I withdrew from the usual holiday gatherings. I stayed home and cooked his favorite meal linguine with clams, anchovies, parmesan, and a splash of Chianti. I sat in silence. I grieved. I felt. I let it wash over me, the sadness, the memories, the love.

That stillness brought healing. For the loss of my father and for the unresolved loss of my brother years ago.

When my sister passed, just one year after my father, I wasn't sure I could handle the planning and organizing all over again. But it was not my time to mourn. It was time to pull things together for her daughters and for my mother.

Afterwards, when I travelled back home, I chose stillness again. It wasn't easy but it was sacred. Stillness became my way back to myself.

Now, every morning, I sit on my bright pink and gold meditation cushion and begin my day with a recitation of thanks. Sometimes they're new and different.

Mass cards for each lost family member are on my altar for a morning hello, and the warmth of reflection and remembrance.

Gratitude has become a daily practice for all that I have. Not what I've lost.

- I give thanks for the gift of three healthy children who live independently and have loving relationships.
- I give thanks for my parents who offered me their very best every day.
- I give thanks for having a brother and a sister (and I miss them both dearly).
- I give thanks for my family, both born and chosen, who enrich my life with presence, laughter, and support.
- I give thanks for my Nespresso® machine, greeting me each morning with comfort and warmth.
- I give thanks for my bed, soft pillows, cozy sheets, and heavy blankets.
- I give thanks for the sun rising over the ocean, painting the day in light.
- I give thanks for my strong and healthy body, and for the ease with which it moves on the yoga mat.
- I give thanks for another day, a blank canvas filled with divine possibility.

- I give thanks for the breath that fills my lungs.
- I give thanks for the beauty I carry, inside and out.
- I give thanks for the clients I serve today and the clients I am calling in tomorrow.

This isn't just a routine. It's a reminder that no matter what I've lost, my life is already full. Gratitude brings me home to myself every single morning.

Turning Grief Into Gratitude

Loss leaves a mark but it can also leave meaning. Gratitude doesn't erase grief, but it reshapes the way we hold it. This chapter is an invitation to explore how deep sorrow can coexist with sacred remembering. Gratitude becomes the thread that gently weaves pain into purpose, and absence into deeper presence.

Reflect

Sit honestly with your grief, not to fix it, but to face it with tenderness. Sometimes what lingers is not just sadness. It's love that has nowhere to go. By revisiting loss through a lens of appreciation, you begin to see that even in the end something beautiful can remain.

- What is one loss that brings grief in you, whether new or long buried?
- What part of that experience still lives in you: as a value, a memory, a lesson, or a sense of who you've become?
- How might you honor the love and meaning that remains, even with the absence?

Journaling Prompt: *What did this loss teach me about love, life, or presence and how can I live in honor of it today?*

Reframe

Reframing allows you to see that gratitude allows grief some space to breathe. You're not being asked to be thankful for the pain, but to be thankful through it. The most difficult chapters in our lives often contain the deepest invitations into wisdom, compassion, and clarity.

- Gratitude doesn't ignore grief, it softens grief.
- Every goodbye carries a hidden blessing waiting to be acknowledged and lived forward.
- What if the most painful parts of your story are the most sacred, because of how they shaped you?

Mantra: *I hold my sorrow in one hand and my gratitude in the other. Both are true. Both are holy.*

Reconnect

The recipients of your gratitude are not just a list. They're a lens. As you remember what shaped you, grief looks less like a burden and more like a bridge.

- **Start a Daily Gratitude Ritual**
  Keep it simple: each morning, write down 3–5 things you're grateful for: people, sensations, comforts, insights.

- **Write a Letter of Thanks**
  Choose someone who shaped you, even if they're no longer living. Write to them. Speak the gratitude you never got to express.

- **Bless the Ordinary**
  Choose one simple item in your life and bless it each day. Let it become a moment of sacred appreciation.

Affirmation: *I carry my grief with grace. I honor what was, and give thanks for what remains. In gratitude, I heal.*

Final Thought: Gratitude is the Bridge Between What Was and What Is

Loss visits every life.
Loss does not steal light.
Loss deepens the soul.
Loss expands your capacity.

Gratitude is a choice.
Gratitude rises with grace.
Gratitude holds joy gently.
Gratitude holds pain too.

Give thanks for what was.
Give thanks for what remains.
Beauty lives in both places.
Beauty continues becoming.

You are not your losses.
You are your returning love.
You are your open heart.
You rise again and again.

This is Sovereign Living.

SCARCITY TO ABUNDANCE

> *"Acknowledging the good that you already have in your life is the foundation for all abundance."*
> ~ Eckhart Tolle

When scarcity creeps in, when it feels like there's not enough time, money, love, or success, the most powerful shift you can make is deceptively simple:

Look around. Acknowledge. Give thanks.

Lack thrives on comparison and fear. Abundance grows from gratitude and belief. Instead of envying someone else's success, admire them. Bless what they have. Celebrate what it must have taken to arrive where they are.

What you admire in others, you invite into your life. Energy follows attention. Fear, scarcity, and lack expands. Celebrate abundance, and more flows to meet you. It's not magic. It's alignment. It's not fantasy. It's frequency.

My Story: A Personal Lesson in Abundance

When I was 15, I bought my first car outright, with no loan and no gift, using money I earned from part-time jobs. I even saved enough to pay for my own driving lessons, determined to drive myself to work by my 16th birthday.

There was no big strategy. No five-year plan. Just work, save, and earn freedom.

With every milestone, however small, I felt rich. Not because of how much I had, but because I valued every single thing I earned.

Later, after our third child was born, our little home started to feel tight: three bedrooms, one and a half baths. It would've been easy to feel frustration. Instead, I began to see the next house in my mind. More space. More love. More room to grow.

I became laser focused on locating a home in one of the very few "trick or treat" neighborhoods in our community. Halloween was a distinct childhood holiday and memory. I was deeply compelled to offer this experience to my children.

And I found it, because I believed it was possible and I acted in alignment with that belief.

Coincidentally (or not) a salary increase came shortly after the closing. That's abundance, not excess. It's expanding from the inside out.

Cultivating Scarcity to Sacred Plenty

Scarcity begins in the mind, not the bank account or calendar. It's shaped by fear, comparison, and conditioning. Abundance is not something you chase. It's something you choose to see, feel, and embody.

Reflect

Scarcity doesn't always mean absence. Sometimes it's disconnection: from presence, from trust, from the truth that abundance already exists within and around you.

- Where are you currently experiencing scarcity? In time, love, money, creativity, opportunity?
- What story are you telling yourself about what's missing?
- Is this story rooted in fact? Or in fear, comparison, or old conditioning?

Journaling Prompt: *What would shift if I stopped focusing on what I don't have and started blessing what I do?*

Reframe

Reframing allows you to see that lack is not always reality; it's often perception. What you focus on multiplies. When you choose gratitude, you amplify awareness. And where there is awareness, there is abundance waiting to be received.

- Lack is a feeling, not a fact. Feelings can change with perspective.
- What you bless, grows. What you resent, repels.
- When you honor what already exists, that energy attracts what's aligned.

Mantra: *I live in the flow of enough. What I seek is already seeking me.*

Reconnect

Reconnection is about turning your attention from fear to faith and aligning your energy with the abundance you desire. It isn't about pretending. It's about embodying as if you are already resourced, already connected, already free. Because in many ways you are.

- **Visualize Your Expansion**
  Choose one area of scarcity. Close your eyes and imagine that part of your life is already full. Feel it. Breathe it. Let all your systems register it as real.

- **Celebrate Abundance in Others**
  When you see someone really thriving, celebrate them. Their gain is not your loss. Let their success stretch your capacity to receive.

- **Practice "As If"**
  Move, speak, and make decisions from your abundant self. Dress like it. Walk like it. Choose with confidence. Show the universe you're already living aligned with what you're calling in.

Affirmation: *I release the story of not enough. I am deeply supported. I am already in abundance and it continues to grow.*

Final Thought: What You Bless, Blesses You Back

Abundance begins with reverence.
Reverence for what is here now.
Bless the life in your hands.
Watch new blessings rush toward you.

You are not behind, beloved.
You are not broken.
You are not lacking.
You are already overflowing within.

You are ready to receive.
You are full of quiet riches.
You are blooming into more.
You are becoming your own abundance.

Live from this softened knowing.
Let gratitude open every door.
Life meets you where you rise.
What you bless returns in beauty.

This is Sovereign Living.

CLUTTERED MIND TO LASER-FOCUSED DESIRE

*"When you really want something,
the universe conspires to
help you to achieve it."*
~ Paulo Coelho

Many people have dreams. Few people turn them into reality. What's the difference? Focus. Intention. A plan.

Fulfilled creators design. They live with clarity about what matters most, rooted in how they want to feel, and committed to meaningful, intentional steps.

Envision the desire, clarify the feeling, create a plan, trust the unfolding. When your energy is scattered, so are your results. But when you move from the inside out with a clear focus, the universe matches your momentum.

My Story: From Vision Board to Synchronicity

Following our marital separation I was sitting peacefully in my new home with a quiet sense of anticipation. I felt called to create a new vision board, an updated map of what I wanted to manifest.

Before I began, my dear friend Kimberly suggested I read *The Desire Map* by Danielle LaPorte. That book changed everything. I realized desire isn't just about external things. It's about how you want to feel.

I dove into her five core life areas:

- Livelihood & Lifestyle
- Body & Wellness

- Creativity & Learning
- Relationships & Society
- Essence & Spirituality

Instead of chasing outcomes, I began to ask how I wanted to feel in each area of my life. Then my energy shifted. I stopped scattering a thousand ideas and saw what I wanted to experience every day:

Balance in all I do.

Freedom to be who I am and who I am becoming.

Luxuriousness in experiences that stimulate all my senses.

Connection to others; family, friends, colleagues and community.

Intimacy and depth in relationships. Quality over quantity.

Then came the synchronicity. Two years later, I attended the Amazing Woman Entrepreneur (AWE) event at Wanderlust Hollywood. Danielle was on stage, radiating truth. Later I introduced myself and invited her to speak at the wellness resort I was consulting for, in Costa Rica.

A week later, at Yoga Journal LIVE in Florida, we crossed paths again at her book signing. She remembered me and encouraged me to speak boldly and own my full, feminine power.

I walked away with a crystal-clear message: Get clear. Own your desires. Speak them into existence. And I've been doing so ever since.

Focus on How You Want to Feel

We're taught to chase titles, timelines, outcomes. But behind every desire is a deeper longing: to feel a certain way. When you clarify the feeling beneath the goal, you align with your truth, not just your to-do list.

Reflect

Reflection invites you to question what you're working toward. Is it rooted in who you are or who you think you should be? It's a mistake to pursue goals shaped by others' values. When you know how you actually want to feel, the path forward becomes more honest and more alive.

- What do you really want right now, in your career, your relationships, health, and in your self-expression?
- Are your goals based on external standards or internal resonance?
- Beneath the surface of what you want, what feeling are you after?

Journaling Prompt: *If I could feel anything without earning it what would I choose?*

Reframe

You don't need all the answers. You do need emotional clarity. When you understand how you want to feel, your decisions shift from wanting to receiving. You become a magnet for experiences that reflect your truth.

- You don't need the whole plan. You just need to know how you want to feel.
- Perfection isn't the point, resonance is.
- Clarity doesn't come from thinking harder. It comes from moving with intention and adjusting as you go.

Mantra: *I lead with how I want to feel. My desires are rooted in truth, not performance.*

Reconnect

Get back to your emotional compass, the inner knowing that tells you what is aligned, expansive, and true. When you understand the feeling you're chasing and live as if it's already available, you shift your energy from longing to embodiment.

- **Choose One Core Desire**
  Write it down, then ask:
  – "Why do I want this?"
  – "What feeling am I really after?"

- **Take One Aligned Action Today**
  It can be a phone call, a wardrobe change, or a boundary reset. Let it be in service of a feeling, not just the goal.

- **Create a Vision Around the Feeling**
  – Make a mini vision board or journal entry based on that emotion, not the outcome.
  – Let the feeling shape your visuals and words: calm, excitement, freedom, presence and love.

Affirmation: *I honor how I want to feel. I choose aligned action over approval. My desires are sacred, and they begin with me.*

Final Thought: Desire with Direction is Magnetic

When your focus becomes clear, you shift.
When desire aligns with soul, you expand.
You stop chasing so hard.
You begin attracting with ease.

You no longer force your life.
Your life rises from within.
Flow replaces pressure.
Grace replaces striving.

You were not born for perfection.
You were born for passion.
You were born for fire.
You were born for rhythm.

Let desire guide your steps.
Let alignment ground your becoming.
Let your life reveal its masterpiece.
Let your magnetism lead the way.

This is Sovereign Living.

Pro Tip:

I highly recommend picking up *The Desire Map* and the companion workbook, and/or signing up for Danielle LaPorte's course at OneCommune.com.

Your soul and your future self will thank you.

DISTRACTION TO INTENTIONAL ACTION

"The 5 Second Rule: The moment you have an instinct to act on a goal you must 5-4-3-2-1 and physically move or your brain will stop you."
~ Mel Robbins

Modern life pulls you in a hundred directions. It's easy to confuse movement with momentum. But being busy is not the same as being purposeful. Distraction depletes. Intention energizes. The antidote to chaos is intentional action.

When your day begins with clarity, rooted in your core desires, your energy becomes sacred. You stop reacting and start creating. This is how you move from simply filling up your time to truly fulfilling your life.

My Story: A Sacred Morning Ritual

As someone who thrives on productivity and forward motion, I used to begin my days with rapid-fire urgency. Emails. Texts. And that daily 7:00am real estate client phone call. By noon I had crossed off half my to-do list. But I often felt scattered and strangely unsatisfied.

Eventually, I learned that if I didn't direct my energy with intention, the world would claim it for itself.

That's why I now begin each evening with intention. Before bed, I brew a cup of tea and journal my priorities for the following day. I categorize them into three areas:

- Personal
- Professional
- Soul-centered

Each morning, after I wake, I use Mel Robbins's *The 5 Second Rule* to ignite the day. I sip coffee slowly. I roll out my yoga mat and devote time to gratitude, breath work, light movement, and inspirational listening.

Only after I'm grounded do I move toward my deepest work, which is often writing. Some days, the words flow freely. Other days, resistance creeps in. When that happens, I pivot. I move my body, breathe more deeply, and shift to a different meaningful task.

But always, my day begins anchored in purpose, not pressure.

Claiming the Day Before It Claims You

Your day doesn't begin when the alarm goes off, it begins when your attention is focused. The choices you make, especially in the early moments, either align you with purpose or reactively scatter your thoughts in reaction. You need to shift from autopilot to intention, from distraction to devotion. You don't need more hours in your day. You need more alignment with what matters.

Reflect

Reflection helps you notice where your time, focus, and energy are flowing. Presence is a practice. Mindful ownership of your day starts with one honest check-in at a time.

- Do you begin your day with intention or do you immediately react to outside demands?
- What are your most frequent distractions? What do they cost you mentally, emotionally, and energetically?
- When during your day do you naturally feel most focused, energized, and clear?

Journaling Prompt: *If I were to honor what matters most, how would I shape the first hour of my day?*

Reframe

Stop labeling yourself as "unfocused" or "all over the place." Proactive discipline rooted in desire and devotion becomes freedom. Clarity without hustle is equal to productivity.

- You're not "bad at focus." You've simply been stretched in too many directions without a sacred anchor.
- Discipline isn't about force, it's about devotion to what deeply matters.
- You don't need more time, you need more clarity about what deserves your attention.

Mantra: *My presence is powerful. My day is shaped by what I choose to honor.*

Reconnect

Reconnection is about aligning action with intention every day. When you pause to choose what matters before the day chooses for you, you regain your Sovereignty. Even small shifts create big momentum.

- **Set Tomorrow in Motion Tonight**
  Before bed, write down your top three priorities for the next day. Let clarity arrive before the chaos.

- **Taking Action** *(The 5 Second Rule)*
  Upon waking up, instead of lying in bed and obsessing about a topic, count down 5-4-3-2-1 and physically move your body out of bed before the five seconds are up.

- **Protect the First Hour**
  – Keep your phone on airplane mode.
  – Light a candle, breathe, stretch, journal, or simply sit with your thoughts.
  – Let your energy lead, not your notifications.

- **Devote 15 Uninterrupted Minutes**
  Choose the one task or dream you've been avoiding. Set a timer and begin. Just the act getting started shifts your momentum.

Affirmation: *I honor my energy by choosing with intention. Each mindful act shapes a life I am proud to live.*

Final Thought: You Are the Keeper of Your Energy

Your energy is sacred currency.
Every distraction spends it quickly.
Every intention invests it wisely.
Your power begins with awareness.

You are not here to react.
You are here to move purposefully.
You are here to walk with peace.
You are here to live in rhythm.

Begin your day anchored deeply.
Let the world soften around you.
Lead with luminous clarity.
Life will answer with alignment.

Busyness is noise you outgrow.
Presence is power you embody.
Guard what your eyes receive.
Let your energy lead your life.

This is Sovereign Living.

OBSESSION WITH AN IDEA TO PLANTING THE SEED OF DESIRE

> *"Desires are seeds waiting for their season to sprout. From a single seed of desire, whole forests grow."*
> ~ *Deepak Chopra*

According to the law of attraction, our thoughts hold the power to shape reality. When we sync our mindset with our deepest desires, we become magnets to the life we envision.

Desire is powerful, but obsession strangles growth. When you hold too tightly and have too many expectations, you create resistance. Manifestation flows from trust. When you plant a seed and surrender the timeline, life will surprise you in extraordinary ways.

My Story: From Dreaming to Living by the Sea

Growing up in New York and then raising my children in Connecticut, the beach was always just a short drive away. I longed not just to visit the ocean, but to live beside it.

After my youngest daughter graduated from high school, someone asked me, "What will you do next?"

I instantly replied, "I'm going to live near the beach, where the sun shines every day." It wasn't a plan. It was a knowing.

In mid-August, just an hour after dropping Maddie off at college, my phone rang. It was a longtime friend, a builder: "Are you ready to move to Fairfield Beach? I have a project and I need your help." I responded with a resounding, *"Yes!"*

Six months later, on Valentine's Day I purchased a charming beach house on stilts. There were endless views of the Long Island Sound to the east, to the west and south. The daily sunsets were extraordinary.

But life had an even bigger surprise waiting.

Three months later, at the completion of a week-long yoga retreat in Costa Rica, the owner of Rythmia Life Advancement Center approached me.

"Come work for me," he said.
"I'm not a yoga teacher," I laughed.
"I'm a Marketing Director."
"Exactly," he smiled. "That's what I need."

By Monday afternoon, I had resigned from my high paying salary and corporate role. Two weeks later, I relocated again, this time to Malibu, CA. A place where the sun shines every day, where the ocean is a few steps away, and where my dreams expanded beyond anything I could have imagined.

The lesson? Manifestation doesn't require control. It requires clarity, trust, and openness to how life wants to bless you.

Planting a Seed and Letting It Bloom in Its Own Time

Every desire is a seed. But growth takes patience, presence, and trust. Too often we try to force results, mistaking urgency for faith. You are not here to control every outcome. You are here to co-create with grace.

Reflect

Reflection invites you to acknowledge the desire that's been quietly within you, maybe for years. Has it been nurtured with care, or afflicted with tension? True manifestation begins with listening and patience.

- What is one deep desire you've carried in your heart for years without letting go?
- Have you been gently nurturing this desire, or anxiously obsessing over it?
- Can you remember a moment when life surprised you with something far better than what you were trying to control?

Journaling Prompt: *What desire am I ready to trust again not with pressure, but with patience and presence?*

Reframe

When you release the need to control the "how" and "when," you begin to walk in alignment instead of anxiety. Clarity invites. Desperation repels. Growth needs space.

- Desire is magnetic. Desperation is resistant.
- You don't have to chase. You only need to clarify your vision, align your actions, and trust the unfolding.
- Let go of controlling the how and when. Let life co-author the journey. Let it delight you.

Mantra: *I plant the seed in trust. I water it with presence. I release the timeline.*

Reconnect

Tend to your desires like a gardener. You do your part and then allow the sun, soil, and seasons to do theirs. You don't manifest through force. You manifest through alignment, belief, and daily acts of faith.

- **Revisit One Core Desire**
  Ask Yourself: "How does this desire serve your highest good and the good of others?"

- **Live in the Energy of Already Having It**
  Embody the outcome before it arrives. Dress for it. Speak from it. Make choices aligned with your future self.

- **Surround Yourself With Expansive Energy**
  Be with people who stretch your thinking, support your vision, and remind you what's possible, not just what's practical.

Affirmation: *My desires are seeds of destiny. I plant with intention, water with love, and trust what will bloom.*

Final Thought: The Art of Sacred Manifestation

Manifestation is co-creation.
You plant each seed with clarity.
You plant each dream with devotion.
The universe responds with grace.

Timing becomes your ally.
Mystery becomes your companion.
Grace becomes your nourishment.
Everything unfolds in rhythm.

Tend the soil of belief.
Prepare yourself for harvest.
Trust the sacred process.
Trust the wisdom of your soul.

Blooming has its season.
Receiving has its moment.
Your readiness opens the door.
Your faith calls the future forward.

This is Sovereign Living.

RESISTANCE TO PERSISTENCE

"Persistence overcomes resistance."
~ Mark Victor Hansen

This may seem obvious, but do not resist the very thing you are trying to attract. Don't get in your own way. Be persistent. Stay devoted to your vision without overthinking why it hasn't arrived, blaming yourself, or doubting the process.

Persistence means moving forward with faith, even when tangible results are not yet visible. There's a silent agreement between you and the universe that says: "I trust you. I trust myself. I trust the timing."

Your energy becomes magnetic when you move forward persistently and courageously, no matter how long the path may seem.

When you hit a difficult patch, confront the invisible belief barriers. Ask yourself:

- "Do I believe in this more than those who doubt?"
- "Will I hold my vision steady even when others can't see it?"

Your limitations exist only in the mind. Think bigger. Trust deeper. Persist longer.

My Story: Persistence in Action

I have a real estate client who dreams of returning to Malibu, her soul's true home. Although her financial situation is secure, personal responsibilities have made the timing complicated.

We persist. We monitor the market. We visit homes in Malibu. We educate ourselves on trends. We nourish the dream.

Each time she apologizes for not making a move yet, I reassure her that the act of showing up, learning, and envisioning is progress in itself. The universe is listening. And when the right home appears and the timing is right, she will be ready.

Persistence, paired with patience, always prevails.

The Power of Gentle Devotion

Persistence isn't always loud or forceful. Often it's quiet, rhythmic, and rooted. In a world that glorifies immediate results, it's easy to misread delays as denials. Soul-led goals require a different pace. So shift from resistance to rhythm. Choose steady devotion over self-doubt. What's meant for you responds to your consistency, not your control.

Reflect

When have you expected results to come quickly and then abandoned the process when they didn't? Lasting growth is built in seasons, not sprints.

- Where in your life have you mistaken delay for denial?
- Do you give up if results don't arrive quickly or do you trust the long game?
- What vision, project, or dream in your life right now deserves more of your presence and persistence?

Journaling Prompt: *Where am I being asked to stay the course, not with pressure, but with presence?*

Reframe

Resistance isn't a red light, it's a request to reframe and realign. Every dream worth having requires moments of waiting, recalibrating, and trusting. When you show up consistently, even imperfectly. you prove your faith to the dream itself.

- Resistance is not a stop sign, its a signal to return to alignment.

- Your dream is not too big. Your timeline is not too late.

- Progress isn't about doing it all today. It's about moving forward.

Mantra: *I am devoted, not desperate. I move forward, one aligned step at a time.*

Reconnect

Reconnection is the practice of persistently staying connected to your vision. You don't have to force the outcome. You only have to keep showing up. The effects of small, daily actions are immensely powerful. That's how momentum begins and continues.

- **Dedicate 15 Minutes Each Morning to Your Vision**
  Visualize, sketch, plan, take action. The habit creates the path.

- **Replace Frustration With Faith**
  Say aloud: "What I seek is also seeking me."
- **Keep Showing Up**
  You don't have to "feel like it" every day. You only have to honor the dream with your presence. Quiet devotion builds more momentum than bursts of pressure.

Affirmation: *I persist with grace. I trust the unfolding. I honor my dreams with steady love, not urgency.*

Final Thought: Gentle Devotion Outlasts Resistance

Persistence overcomes resistance every time.
Do not resist what you desire.
Stay devoted without forcing outcomes.
Trust timing more than urgency.

Move forward even without visible results.
Faith grows through consistent action.
Your energy becomes quietly magnetic.
Courage compounds when you keep going.

Resistance is not a stop sign.
It is a call to realign.
Delays are not denials.
They are invitations to deepen trust.

Progress comes through steady presence.
Devotion outlasts doubt and fear.
Show up with grace daily.
What's meant for you will respond.

This is Sovereign Living.

BIRD'S EYE VIEW TO SPY PLANE VIEW

"Your attitude, not your aptitude, will determine your altitude."

~ Zig Ziglar

We've all heard the term "view from 30,000 feet." It means stepping back to gain clarity, to organize, realign, and prioritize.

There's an even higher vantage point. It's the view at 70,000 feet where spy planes fly and vision isn't just broad, it's borderless.

At that level you can design your future. You see hidden patterns, potentials, and pitfalls. You're no longer reacting. You're leading with intention and elevation.

Just as spy planes are built for reconnaissance, you can train yourself to gather insight, spot opportunity, and see the difference between drama and discernment.

From the spy plane altitude, your life becomes a strategy in which your values, goals, and actions acquire elegant precision.

My Story: When a New View Changed Everything

For many years on New Year's Day, my dear friend Kimberly and I sit down with glue sticks, stacks of magazines, and a bottle of sparkling water, with a side of hot tea to make vision boards. On January 1, 2025, I was visiting Kimberly in Connecticut and I had four intentions in mind:

- Deepen relationships with my adult children
- Double my business income
- Maintain physical vitality
- Travel to a new region of Italy

Halfway through clipping images, Kimberly turned to me and asked, "Would you ever leave your real estate agency?"

Without hesitation, I said, "No, I would not." I was sure I was exactly where I needed to be.

But six days later, while I was still in Connecticut, the Palisades Fire tore through Malibu. Would my apartment survive? Miraculously, it did. with only smoke damage. (And by the grace of God this book's manuscript was also saved!)

Still, the experience shook me. Back in California, as I moved around from hotels to an Airbnb to finally landing a temporary beachside bungalow, a question kept rising: *What if I'm being nudged higher?*

Then came an invitation from COMPASS, the #1 real estate agency in Malibu, So Cal, and even in the whole country. At first, I declined. Comfort and habit blurred my view.

But when I rose to my spy plane level, I saw the opportunity as a perfect match for my values; a wider platform for the clients I serve; and greater alignment with my long-term goals.

Within two weeks, I made the move. It wasn't in my original plan. It was better. And with heartfelt gratitude for the agency that trained me, supported me, and gave me my first foundation, I carried their lessons with respect as I stepped into a new season of expansion.

Elevate Your Vision and Soar High

Sometimes, the breakthrough isn't in doing more. It's seeing from a greater height. True vision comes from elevation, from rising above "what is" to discover "what could be." Elevate your altitude, shift your vantage point, and gain the clarity that comes from rising.

Reflect

Reflection asks you to examine your current "big picture." Is it truly expansive or just a bit larger than what feels safe? Have you been zooming out, but not up? Don't miss opportunities by viewing your path through old filters.

- Where are you operating from a 30,000-foot view when you could go even higher?
- Is your current "big picture" your highest self, or in past assumptions, old desires, or self-imposed limitations?
- What would become possible if you saw your life, your work, your purpose from a higher perspective?

Journaling Prompt: *What have I been viewing from the ground and what might shift if I saw it from above?*

Reframe

Reframing invites you to understand that vision is not a gift for the chosen, it's power for the committed. When you elevate your perspective, you access clarity that simply isn't available from a lower level. You recognize what matters and release what doesn't.

- 70,000 feet is not out of reach. It's a practice of stepping back, rising above, and daring to dream beyond what's visible now.
- What looks like chaos at ground level becomes coherence from above.
- The next-level vision you're waiting for isn't out of reach. It's waiting for you to rise up and meet it.

Mantra: *I rise for clarity. I lead from vision. I return grounded in purpose.*

Reconnect

You don't elevate by accident. You elevate through pause, presence, and perspective. Give yourself space to dream higher, think clearer, and return with renewed direction.

- **Create a Personal Offsite**
  – Once a month, block off a full day for seeing the whole picture. No errands. No emails. Just you, and your future.
  – Ask big questions. Let yourself imagine beyond the now.

- **Revisit a Stalled Goal**
  Ask Yourself:
  – "What would this look like from 70,000 feet?"
  – "What are the patterns?"
  – "What's the bigger opportunity?"
  – "What would the highest version of yourself choose to do?"

- **Use Mantra as Meditation**
  Sit quietly and repeat: "I rise above for wisdom, and return to earth with power." Let your breath match the rhythm of your vision.

Affirmation: *I see from above, I lead with vision. I align with elevation and act with grounded grace.*

Final Thought: The Altitude of Sovereignty

At seventy thousand feet, the noise fades.
From this height, life becomes choreography.
Nothing feels random anymore.
Everything reveals its preparation.

Elevation widens your awareness.
You stop reacting to circumstance.
You begin responding with wisdom.
Clarity becomes your new perspective.

From this altitude, fear grows small.
Purpose glows luminous and steady.
Vision replaces worry entirely.
Alignment replaces exhausting effort.

You architect your own horizon.
You lead your life with grace.
Let your vision rise higher.
Let your choices match your altitude.

This is Sovereign Living.

PESSIMISM TO OPTIMISM

> *"Optimism isn't a belief that things will automatically get better. It's a conviction to make them better."*
> ~ *Melinda French Gates*

Is the glass half empty or half full? Will this moment lead to frustration or to joy?

Science tells us that nearly 80% of our thoughts are negative, and 95% are repetitive. Most of our thinking is unhelpful and habitual. Left unchecked, our thoughts default to fear, comparison, self-criticism, and doubt.

But you're not just a product of neurology. You're a Sovereign soul. Optimism is a choice you can always make.

Optimism doesn't ignore the facts. It reframes them with faith, intention, and vision. It moves you from helpless to powerful. From reactive to creative. From limitation to possibility.

My Story: Choosing Optimism Over Disappointment

After my marital separation, I began dating a man who loved art and museums. For his birthday, I planned a special day in New York City. Every detail was thoughtfully crafted, a private driver, gallery stops, dinner reservations, so we could celebrate joyfully before returning back to Connecticut that night.

One highlight was the Henri Matisse exhibit at MoMA.

But when we arrived, the exhibit was completely sold out. My heart sank.

I stepped into the restroom, looked into the mirror, and asked myself, *How do I want the rest of this visit to go?* I took a deep breath and chose a new frame: *There must be tickets somewhere that are meant just for us.*

I walked back to the counter and shared our story: his birthday, our travel, his mother's love for Matisse. The agent smiled and handed us two tickets.

Amazingly enough, the following year in Paris, at the largest Monet exhibition ever curated, we learned it was completely sold out.

Okay. *But once again, there have to be tickets out there just for us.*

After a quick conversation with the hotel concierge, we learned of a little-known secret: the museum released a handful of tickets early each morning, first come, first served. The odds were slim. We'd have to get there really early and wait.

So we did. In the cold Paris rain, we stood in line for an hour, hopeful and shivering. And it paid off. We witnessed the totally breathtaking Monet collection. An unforgettable, once-in-a-lifetime event we almost missed. But those tickets were waiting just for us!

Living in the Frequency of Favor

In a world that often primes us to expect the worst, choosing to believe in the best is a revolutionary practice. So join the revolution. Expect support, invite alignment, and move through uncertainty with a spirit that knows the best outcome is unfolding.

Reflect

Optimism isn't a delusion, it's a decision. Even before the evidence is visible, it's the choice to see life through a lens of support rather than sabotage.

- What has your mind been rehearsing lately, possibility or fear?
- When did you see optimism pay off? If never, start now.
- What would shift if you expected *good news*, not just braced for impact?

Journaling Prompt: *What am I ready to believe is possible again, even if I've stopped saying it out loud?*

Reframe

You don't have to pretend everything is perfect. But you can believe that what's happening is guiding you toward something meaningful. Setbacks can redirect you. Optimism lets you hold on to the bigger picture, even when the current view seems unclear.

- Replace "What if it goes wrong?" with "What if it works out better than I imagined?"
- Setbacks are often setups. You're being positioned, not punished.
- Delay is not denial. It's an invitation to deepen trust, not diminish belief.

Mantra: *What's meant for me is already on its way and it's better than I expected.*

Reconnect

Reconnection is not just hoping things will go well. It's acting as if they already are. Optimism becomes a vibration. A practice. A lens. When you look through it consistently, life starts to respond in kind.

- **Keep a "Proof-of-Possibility" Journal**
  Each day, write down small miracles, aligned moments, unexpected kindness, or new breakthroughs. These are reminders: "Life is working with me."

- **Speak Your Desires Into Existence**
  Say them out loud. Daily. With confidence. Not begging. Believing. Your voice is a tool for alignment.

- **Use This Anchor Mantra When Doubt Creeps In**
  "I trust what is meant for me is already on its way." Repeat this before you act, and when fear begins to whisper.

Affirmation: *I live in the frequency of favor. I expect the best and I open fully to receive it.*

Final Thought: The Frequency of Favor

Optimism is mastery, not naivety.
It is the art of holding light.
It is faith when life feels dim.
It is trust in the unseen.

Even detours are divine.
Every delay carries design.
Belief shifts what becomes possible.
Your thoughts become prayers in motion.

Your outlook becomes your outcome.
Optimism creates the proof it seeks.
It partners with pure potential.
It opens the door to favor.

Trust life is conspiring for you.
Expect goodness rising toward you.
Stand tall in sacred belief.
What you bless becomes more.

This is Sovereign Living.

NO TO A RESOUNDING YES!

"The reflexive 'no' protects us. The conscious 'yes' transforms us."
~ *Author Unknown*

We often say *no* to avoid discomfort. To shield ourselves from risk, judgment, failure, or the unknown. Sometimes it's instinctual. Sometimes it's habitual. And sometimes it's the very thing holding us back from a much larger life.

When *no* becomes a reflex, it shuts the door to magic. Saying *yes* is a radical act of self-trust. It's about recognizing alignment, opportunity, and soul-led expansion. Your soul knows when something is right even if your mind can't explain why.

My Story: Saying Yes to the Unseen

Saying *yes* to marriage was easy.

Saying *yes* to becoming a mother was easy.

But saying yes to uprooting my entire life in Connecticut and leaving a newly purchased beach house for an uncertain role in California took everything I had.

The offer arrived after a powerful weeklong retreat with my daughter at Rythmia Life Advancement Center in Costa Rica. I had just fulfilled a dream two decades in the making: purchasing a charming home on Fairfield Beach Road. Everything felt secure. Comfortable. Settled.

Then came the invitation. "Come work for us," the retreat owner said. My heart fluttered with excitement.

But from the outside the move looked reckless. Friends questioned my sanity. "You just got your dream home. What are you thinking?"

Maddie, wise beyond her years, framed it perfectly: "Mom, it's time for you to go off to college too."

I said *yes*, and that one *yes* changed everything. *Yes* opened doors I hadn't even known were there.

I stepped into the role of Marketing Director at the resort, guided by the powerful insight that women are seeking heart-centered guidance. With that vision, I created a Guest Speaker Program rooted in authenticity and soul. In just one year, we welcomed more than forty world renowned thought leaders, teachers, and spiritual guides into our community.

Below are an example of the Brilliant Souls Who I was Blessed to Say Yes to:

- **Beth Shaw** – Founder of YogaFit, pioneering accessible and healing fitness-based yoga
- **Don Miguel Ruiz & Don Jose Ruiz** – Masters of Toltec wisdom and authors of *The Four Agreements*
- **Dr. Bruce Lipton** – Cellular biologist who proved belief can rewrite DNA
- **Foster & Kimberly Gamble** – Creators of *Thrive*, exploring sustainability and global solutions
- **Dr. Gabor Maté** – Trauma expert connecting emotional pain to lifelong healing
- **Gregg Braden** – Visionary bridging science, spirituality, and human potential

- **John Gray** – Bestselling author of *Men Are from Mars, Women Are from Venus*

- **Mark Victor Hansen & Crystal Dwyer Hansen** – Experts in the power of asking; Mark co-created *Chicken Soup for the Soul*

- **Miranda Macpherson** – Spiritual teacher guiding souls toward grace through surrender

- **Rev. Michael Bernard Beckwith** – Founder of Agape Spiritual Center, empowering global spiritual awakening

- **Shauna Shapiro** – Leading mindfulness researcher and author

- **Shiva Rea** – Lifelong yogini and creator of Prana Vinyasa, the yoga of breath and flow

None of these life-changing conversations would have happened if I'd said *no*.

Saying Yes to the Soul's Invitation

Not every opportunity deserves your energy, but some are sacred invitations to grow, expand, and step deeper into alignment. Knowing when to say *yes* is not about pressure or performance; it's about resonance. Accept the invitation to tune in, trust your inner knowing, and courageously respond when life offers you something that calls your name.

Reflect

Notice how your body and spirit react when something meaningful arises. A *yes* might not feel easy, but it feels alive. It hums a melody beneath the uncertainty. It's not just, "Can I do this?" Instead it's, "This moves me closer to the person I'm becoming."

- When have you felt pulled toward something, but hesitated?
- What physical sensations show up in your body when something is a true *yes*. Expansion? Warmth? Excitement?
- Can you name a time you said *yes* and it changed you? Or when saying *no* brought regret?

Journaling Prompt: *What opportunities or desires have I quietly wanted to say yes to but haven't trusted myself to claim yet?*

Reframe

Reframing allows a shift from overthinking to inner listening. A true *yes* may challenge you, but it won't betray you. The most aligned path may feel scary because it's new, not because it's wrong.

- Saying *yes* isn't about being ready. It's about being *willing*.
- A true yes might scare you, but it also excites you.
- Instead of asking "Can I do this?" ask *"Does this align with who I'm here to become?"*

Mantra: *I trust what lights me up. My yes is sacred, and I follow it with courage.*

Reconnect

When you say *yes* from truth, you activate momentum. You step into flow. You let life meet you in your willingness. Saying *yes* isn't about having the whole plan. It's about trusting the next step.

- **Revisit a Desire or Opportunity You've Been Avoiding**
  – Ask Yourself: "Is this stretching me or steering me away from myself?"
  – If it expands and excites you, move toward it.

- **Speak Your Yes Out Loud**
  Claim it. Let your voice carry your commitment. "This is for me. I say yes."

- **Support Your Yes With Aligned Action**
  – Make the call.
  – Register for the thing.
  – Block time.
  – Say yes with your calendar, your money, your presence.

Affirmation: *When I say yes to what aligns, life responds with clarity, courage, and grace.*

Final Thought: The Sacred Power of Yes

Every yes creates an unseen ripple.
Every yes opens a new doorway.
Every yes invites your evolution.
Every yes expands your becoming.

A conscious yes reclaims courage.
It tells life you are ready.
It tells destiny you're listening.
It tells your soul you trust.

Yes does not erase fear.
Yes transforms fear into faith.
Yes awakens what was sleeping.
Yes bridges intuition and action.

Your yes is magnetic.
Your yes rearranges universes.
You were born to open fully.
You were born to rise and answer.

This is Sovereign Living.

The Yes Manifesto

Today, I choose to say *yes.*
Yes to growth.
Yes to possibility.
Yes to the unknown paths that call my name.

I say yes to opportunities before I feel fully ready.
Yes to adventures that expand my heart.
Yes to conversations that stretch my mind.
And yes to dreams so big they scare me.

I trust that every yes I give to life,
life will return to me a thousandfold in growth,
joy, and wisdom.

I am open. I am willing. I am brave.
I say yes to the life that is waiting for me beyond fear.

RELEASE TO EXPAND

*"We must be willing to let
go of the life we've planned,
so as to have the life
that is waiting for us".*
~ Joseph Campbell

Letting go is one of the most courageous acts we can commit. We cling to titles, roles, possessions, and relationships. We believe they define us, complete us, protect us. But they only anchor us to who we used to be.

To grow into our next season, we must release what no longer serves us. Not with bitterness, but with gratitude. Not with fear, but with trust.

Releasing is not a loss. It's an offering. A signal to the Universe: I'm ready now. Ready to expand. Ready to evolve. Ready to receive something greater.

We cannot pour new wine into old skins. Expansion begins the moment we choose space over stagnation, clarity over clutter, and faith over fear.

My Story: Clearing the Runway for Flight

Over the past 15 years, I've let go of homes, careers, cars, jewelry, and clothing. Perhaps most difficult of all, I've let go of my ego identity. I've said goodbye to roles that once made me feel important, relationships that once made me feel needed, and zip codes that once made me feel rooted.

It hasn't always been easy. But something remarkable happened: I expanded.

My dear friend Haamid often says, "You dodged a bullet." It's a shorthand for "You released something that was blocking your blessings."

I've embraced mobility and minimalism. My suitcase is always ready. My passport is always near. My energy is unburdened.

I regularly clear out clutter, especially during the new moon. Closets. Drawers. Digital files. Even conversations. If something no longer aligns, I let it go not with resentment but with reverence.

Opportunities, money, people, even love, they come and go. And that's okay. What's meant for me will find me. What's past has taught me. What's coming will also teach me.

This is freedom.
This is flow.
This is **Sovereign Living.**

The Sacred Art of Letting Go

Releasing isn't weakness, it's wisdom. What once served you may now be stalling you. Letting go is not about loss. It's about seeing what's outdated, untangling from what's no longer true, and creating space for a life that fits who you're becoming, not just who you've been.

Reflect

Acknowledge what is still holding on to, and ask whether they reflect your current truth. Weight we carry isn't from what we lack, but from what we haven't yet released.

- What are you still carrying that feels like a burden?
- Is this person, pattern, belief, or role serving your current growth or binding you to a past version of yourself?
- What would you gain energetically, emotionally and spiritually if you chose to release this?

Journaling Prompt: *What am I afraid to release and what am I more afraid of missing if I don't?*

Reframe

Reframing allows you to shift your understanding of release from loss to liberation. You are not betraying your past by evolving. You are honoring your truth by clearing space. Letting go is a sacred form of self-respect.

- Releasing is not rejection. It's a redirect.
- You're not losing. you're lightening.
- Letting go isn't giving up, it's choosing aligned truth over outdated loyalty.

Mantra: *I bless what was. I honor what is. I release to rise.*

Reconnect

Reconnection is making space for new desires asking to emerge. It's also about creating ritual around the release so that it becomes conscious, embodied, and honored. When you let go with intention, you don't just push something into your past. You invite something from your future.

- **Ask What's Now Asking for Space**
  What desire, vision, or part of yourself is ready to grow, if only there were room?

- **Speak With Intention**
  Say aloud: "I am releasing XXX. I am inviting YYY and ZZZ." Let it be a vow, a personal ceremony, a blessing.

- **Honor the Grief**
  – Even letting go of what hurts can feel like a loss.
  – Make space for tears, stillness, or quiet ceremony.
  – Grief is sacred. It clears your soul for what's next.

- **Begin a Gentle Ritual of Release**
  – Write what you're letting go of and burn it (safely).
  – Bury it.
  – Speak it out loud and bless it.
  – Move your body to release stored energy.

- **Envision the New**
  What will feel lighter? Freer? More joyful? Plant that seed today.

- **Practice Radical Self-Compassion**
  – Growth isn't linear. Be gentle with yourself.
  – Releasing takes courage. Integration takes time.

Affirmation: *I trust the wisdom of release. I am clearing space for what is true, light, and mine.*

Final Thought: Expansion Requires Space

You cannot receive with closed hands.
Release is readiness in motion.
Every ending invites evolution.
Every letting go whispers trust.

What you release in love frees you.
What you cling to in fear cages you.
Letting go is liberation embodied.
Letting go is faith made visible.

The universe fills open space.
Make room for what's rising.
Make peace with what's leaving.
Make space for your becoming.

Expansion begins where attachment ends.
The unknown is alive with promise.
Say yes to the clearing.
Say yes to the quiet between chapters.

This is Sovereign Living.

ACKNOWLEDGEMENTS

I'd like to acknowledge the many teachers I've met along the way, around the globe:

Soul Sisters
Kimberly Konstant, Business and Soulbbatical Travel Partner
Lisa Tenore, Yoga Teacher and Divinely Guided Intuitive

Book Co-Creation
Helane Freeman, Design & Layout
Mitch Sisskind, Editor
Sydney Koenig, Photography

Yoga-Mindful Teachers
Alexia Daksha Damini, Alice Khalsa, Bilge Alpay,
Carla Fabre, Chrissy MJ Anderson,
Christopher Tompkins, Colleen Lila Yoga,
Elana Brower, Guru Jagat, Guru Jas Khalsa,
Harijiwan, Harmanjot Kaur, Isa Raim, Parashakti,
Philipp Manser, Ram Kirin, Raquel Griffin,
Sarah Miller: Siri Akasha, Schuyler Grant, Shiva Rea,
Susan Shaner, Teddy Dean, Tej Kaur Khalsa

Guides
Agus Sihman, Ama, Andrea Caresse, Ellen Goldberg,
Ingo Alexander Sohn, Janet Schmidt,
Jessica Kruskamp, June Fagan, Krista Polinsky,
Nicole Rager, Saul, Taita, Tracy Mignon

Thought Leaders & Book Authors
Alan Watts, Barbara Waxman, Brene Brown,
Bruce Feiler, Bruce Lipton, Carol Dweck,
Chip Conley, Crystal and Mark Victor Hansen,
Danielle LaPorte, David Kessler, Deepak Chopra,

Dr. Gabor Maté, Dr. Gary Chapman,
Don Miguel Ruiz, Eckhart Tolle, Elizabeth Gilbert,
Esther Perel, Gabrielle Bernstein, Gregg Braden,
Haamid Dash, Helane Anderson, Iyanla Vanzant,
Jay Rubin, Jay Shetty, Joe Dispenza, John Gray,
Katherine Woodward Thomas,
Leigh and Carla McCloskey, Louise Hay,
Marie Forleo, Mark Nepo, Matthew McConaughey,
Mel Robbins, Michaela Boehm, Norma Kamali,
Paulo Coelho, Reverend Michael Bernard Beckwith,
Rhonda Byrne, Rich Roll, Rob Bell, Shelley Paxton,
Simon Sinek, Vishen Lakhiani and Wayne Dyer

A heartfelt thank you to **Chip Conley**, founder of Modern Elder Academy, and **Gerard Armond Powell**, founder of Rythmia Life Advancement Center.

In beautifully distinct yet equally transformative ways, you each became luminous guides on my journey toward intentional living. Though your paths differ in form, they meet in purpose: a shared devotion to helping others remember who they are and what they are here to become.

Through my years serving as Marketing Director within both of your worlds, I was given a rare privilege: a front-row seat to transformation in its purest form. Chip, your work at Modern Elder Academy reshaped how I view aging, purpose, and wisdom, revealing that elderhood is not a closing chapter but a profound awakening. Gerry, your vision at Rythmia illuminated the sacred union between healing and wholeness, reminding me that freedom begins when the heart comes home to itself.

Your retreats, your teachings, and your unwavering belief in human potential each invited me into deeper truth. You inspired me to live more consciously, to love more courageously, and to help women everywhere reclaim their Sovereignty, their radiant and unshakable sense of self.

I carry the essence of both of your teachings within my own work, grateful for the intersection of grace, grit, and growth that our paths have shared. May we continue to meet in spaces of awakening, wherever hearts gather to remember the sacred truth of who they are.

ABOUT THE AUTHOR

Laura Alfano is the visionary behind *Sovereign Living*, a movement to inspire 20 million women worldwide to reclaim their Crown, Heart and Compass, and to fully embody their power. Born and raised in Port Chester, New York, as the eldest of three, she grew up rooted in the values of faith, perseverance, and family. A natural achiever, she graduated high school early, earned her associate's degree in Fashion Merchandising, and went on to complete a bachelor's degree in Marketing and Management at Pace University.

After college, Laura married, welcomed three healthy children into the world, and raised them while simultaneously building a successful career in marketing with leading consumer packaged goods companies and creative agencies in the NY/CT area. She later transitioned into consulting to create a healthier balance for her family, carrying her instinct for beauty and design into every role she touched.

In 2007, Laura's life was forever altered by the sudden loss of her brother. What began in heartbreak set off a chain reaction of deeper pain and disappointment: the unraveling of her marriage and the painful estrangement from two of her children. Following her losses, Laura embarked on a spiritual journey of self-discovery, a season of exploration and awakening. As a devoted student, she traveled widely, studied various yoga lineages, read extensively in the fields of personal growth, and participated in transformational courses. Even an unplanned plant medicine journey became part of her path toward healing. Through this process, Laura reclaimed her Sovereignty, rediscovering her Crown of self-worth, her Heart of compassion, and her Compass of inner wisdom.

Today, Laura lives seaside in Malibu, California, delighting in her role as mother and grandmother. She is a Luxury Real Estate Advisor, a certified Hatha and Kundalini Yoga teacher and Reiki Master. Out of her personal journey, she created the *Sovereign Living* series of books, workbooks, and inspiration cards; resources designed to help women everywhere embody their worth and rise into lives of beauty, balance, joy, and Sovereignty.

DISCOVER THE SOVEREIGN LIVING COLLECTION

Continue your journey of self-discovery and empowerment with the complete *Sovereign Living* series. Alongside each book, you'll find a companion workbook to help you Reflect, Reframe, and Reconnect, plus a deck of inspiration cards to keep your practice alive every day. Choose one or embrace them all to reclaim your Crown, your Heart, and your Compass.

Sovereign Living I: A Woman's Guide to Reclaiming Your Crown

Sovereign Living I Workbook: Reclaiming Your Crown - Reflect, Reframe, Reconnect

Sovereign Living I Inspiration Cards: Reclaiming Your Crown

Sovereign Living II: A Woman's Guide to Reclaiming Your Heart

Sovereign Living II Workbook: Reclaiming Your Heart - Reflect, Reframe, Reconnect

Sovereign Living II Inspiration Cards: Reclaiming Your Heart

Sovereign Living III: A Woman's Guide to Reclaiming Your Compass

Sovereign Living III Workbook: Reclaiming Your Compass - Reflect, Reframe, Reconnect

Sovereign Living III Inspiration Cards: Reclaiming Your Compass

Workbooks and Inspiration Cards coming as soon as 2026

www.ingramcontent.com/pod-product-compliance
Lightning Source LLC
Chambersburg PA
CBHW041216130526
44582CB00025BA/36